S0-FQN-351

FREEWOMAN

by
Claire Evans

Translated and edited by
Ailsa Hamilton and William Stallybrass

GROSVENOR
LONDON · MELBOURNE · WELLINGTON

First published in French as
Le Défi féminin
by Editions de Caux, Switzerland, 1977
© Editions, Théâtre et Films de Caux SA,
and Robin Evans

Published 1979
by Becket Publications, Oxford

Republished 1986
by Grosvenor Books
54 Lyford Road, London, SW18 3JJ
21 Dorcas Street, South Melbourne, Victoria 3205, Australia
P.O. Box 1834, Wellington, New Zealand
1103 Sunset Avenue, Richmond, Virginia 23221, USA

© Robin Evans 1986
ISBN 0 901269 92 1

Cover design: W Cameron-Johnson
Cover photo: Eric and David Hosking

Typeset by Oxford Publishing Services,
The Studio, Stratford Street, Oxford
Printed in Malta by Interprint Limited

*To Martine,
who was twenty in Paris
in May 1968*

Contents

	Introduction	1
1	Liberation	5
2	Modern Superstitions	9
3	Beast or Beauty	13
4	Fragments of Freud	17
5	Fantastic	23
6	Secret Classroom	28
7	Fried Snowball	34
8	Radical	38
9	For Better For Worse	42
10	A Motherhood Explosion	52
11	Home	59
12	Work?	66
13	One Woman's Europe	72
14	Suffering	79
15	Tomorrow	86

Introduction

There come moments in the life of every society when certain things have to be said, not because they are in keeping with the tide of public opinion, but because that tide is threatening to become a devastating torrent and someone ought to be shouting "Stop!" I am only a woman at home, like millions of other women, but I feel as if I were standing on the bank watching the water reach danger level. What should I do? Shouldn't I shout as loud as I can, and hope that others, whose voices are louder than mine, will take up the cry?

I have been thinking about this book for years. I am Teutonic by blood, French by upbringing and Latin by culture, and now, settled in Britain, I daily imbibe Anglo-Saxon pragmatism and Celtic myth. So I have hopes that my varied angles of thought may find a welcome in a few places.

I have always been interested in the emancipation of women. There is nothing very original in that, especially in my family; my father's three sisters were all pioneer emancipators. The eldest of them, Louise Weiss, in France needs no introduction. She graduated at twenty-one with the highest honours, at a time when few women graduated at all, and then became a political journalist and author, and editor of the review *Europe Nouvelle*. I was a small girl when she organised the campaign in France to obtain political and civic equality for women, including the right to vote. She asked me then to appear with her in a film designed to prove that a woman could take part in politics and still be domesticated. With considerable skill, she made a speech and an omelette in front of the camera, both at the same time. I had to break an egg. All I can remember is that, as usual, I had failed to clean my finger-nails, and the close-ups had to be taken again.

My second aunt was one of the first woman doctors in the Paris hospitals, a pediatrician who later carried out important research into the effects on children of a lack of maternal care. And I can remember the family excitement on the day when the youngest aunt's photograph appeared on the front pages of the newspapers; she had just graduated top from the School of Political Sciences in Paris.

So my childhood ambitions almost inevitably began, "To be the first woman to . . ." My father had been a test pilot; I would be the first woman to fly around the world over the North and South Poles. If my globe has survived in some attic, it must still be marked with the route I chose after lengthy study. Then came the war and the years of Occupation, which were hardly the time for a girl to try to become a pilot. So my ambitions turned to literature: I would be the first woman in the Académie Française. Incidentally, in 1975 — Women's Year — Louise Weiss once again stood as a candidate for the Académie, but the "Immortals" are still exclusively masculine.

When I had graduated from the Sorbonne, the work I finally chose took me into the public and private lives of women in many parts of the world. I have interpreted the public speeches of eminent women from other nations. I have cooked meals for hundreds at a time with women from every continent, from different races and from faraway lands, and discovered the flavour of daily lives in complete contrast to my own. And during many journeys, I must have stayed in the homes of at least 150 families in ten different countries.

Then came my turn to start a home. My husband is English. For the first three years of our marriage, we continued to travel — in North America, Europe, Japan. Afterwards we settled down near Paris, where our son was born, and then in Cambridge. I had rather more time for reading. The status of women was once again a current subject, and I plunged back into it. It was during this time, in the course of the sixties, that the movement for the emancipation of women was replaced by the campaigns for women's liberation. Arianna Stassinopoulos, in her book *The Female Woman*, sums up the difference between the two: "Emancipation insists on equal status for distinctively female roles. Liberation demands the abolition of any such distinctive roles, the achievement of equality through identical patterns of behaviour."[1]

Women's Lib was at first the sphere of intellectuals, journalists and, it must be said, extremists. But press campaign followed upon press campaign, and many ideas which had originally seemed far-fetched were gradually absorbed into the thinking of the public. Not so long ago, to be the mother of a family had been something to be proud of. Suddenly, to be only that was a source of shame.

Two chance conversations made me realise how far things had gone.

A group of us were waiting outside school for the children.

"You won't see me here much longer," said one mother. "I'm starting work tomorrow."

I knew that she had four sons of school age.

"Now that all your children are at school," I said, "perhaps you haven't enough to do at home?"

"No, it isn't that."

"You need more money?"

"No, it isn't that either."

"Perhaps you have a profession you want to take up again?"

"No, not particularly."

"Well?"

"I'm fed up with what the neighbours say."

I was working on a magazine article about families. Finding myself in the company of a young man of twenty-four, I asked him his ideas. He was quite clear: his wife would go out to work and his children would be brought up in a crèche and in successive appropriate institutions.

"Who will teach them not to throw their sweet-papers on the ground?" I asked, remembering that one mother I knew had taken nearly five years to get that lesson into her children's heads. "It's important for the battle against pollution, but who in your institutions will have the time to bother about it?"

The reaction made it quite clear that my question was badly chosen for a young man who had just taken his degree.

Then I said, "The most important thing is, who will answer

their questions?" All mothers know those incongruous but extremely serious questions which children ask, sometimes in the evening when there is time to answer them, sometimes in a piercing little voice in the queue at the supermarket. I quoted a question which my son had asked me recently about Adam and Eve. "Oh," the young man replied, "that's quite simple. There will be tapes, and if a child asks a question about Adam and Eve or about the origin of man, you'll play him the right tape."

This young man is typical of a large number of sincere people, of a level of education considerably above the average and convinced that they are in the spearhead of progress, whose assertions seem to me in complete opposition to what modern science has discovered about evolution and about the psychology of children.

In all this, I have felt for some time that there is a challenge to common sense which women owe it to themselves to take up.

A few weeks ago I had to go to hospital. The surgeon's diagnosis left no doubt. So now I am undertaking this book. A miracle will perhaps allow me to finish it, but in any case I know that I no longer have any excuse for not starting.

Note
[1] Arianna Stassinopoulos: *The Female Woman*, Davis-Poynter, 1973, p. 15.

1
Liberation

You can count on the fingers of one hand the values which are more precious to human beings than life, for which they are prepared not to kill but to die: truth and faith; family, and its extension, country; and freedom. The idea of freedom evokes so deep a response that today no undertaking which requires the allegiance of whole populations is carried out without slogans about freedom. Even in civil wars, one side "defends freedom" while the other "fights for liberation".

The feminist movement is part of this pattern. The catchword "liberation", in many different languages, is on the banners behind which millions of women have started marching, have squatted in ministry corridors and have inundated public opinion with a flood of articles, books and manifestos. There was even a poster in France, advertising kitchen equipment, in which a housewife was throwing her apron to the wind with an air of delight above the caption "Moulinex liberates women".

Ask the leaders of these movements what they aim to liberate their sisters from, and you will never catch them out. The list is long and varied: from sex discrimination, from male exploitation, from economic exploitation, from the grip of taboos, from the slavery of pregnancy, from the monotony of housework, and so on and on.

And the method of gaining this liberation is simple. You claim rights: the right to divorce, the right to work, the right to free contraception and abortion, the right to a state salary for housework, the right to sexual freedom, and so, again, on and on.

Liberated *from* what is clear. Liberated *for* what is less clear. Generally the reply is: to grow, to fulfil yourself, to develop your gifts, to realise your potential. For many women, particularly and perhaps exclusively in the West, "to fulfil yourself" has become the aim of existence. This ought to have resulted in a creative explosion, in a joyous blossoming of personalities as varied as the flowers in spring. Let's be honest — is that what has happened? Not in theory, but in the faces in the street and the underground?

A doctor friend said to me, not without a touch of humour, "When a human being is five per cent self-centred, he is ineffective; at fifteen per cent, he is unhappy; at eighty-five per cent, he is locked up in a psychiatric ward. And they want to make us believe that to be totally self-centred, and do what we like when we like, would be a huge advance for mankind!"

But if that is not the goal, what is? How do we find out? And how do we get there?

I do not know if our mothers and grandmothers were better women than we are; I doubt it. We are probably very much like them. But their path was marked with clear signposts: "straight ahead", "slippery slope", "dead-end", "danger", "good" this way, "bad" that way. The woman who wanted to "go straight" had only to follow the signs. The woman who wanted to leave the straight road knew what to expect. In the course of the twentieth century these signposts have been taken away one by one. More and more people are coming to believe in all sincerity that there is no road and no goal, and that good and evil have disappeared along with the signposts.

There is one thing to do if you find yourself in unknown territory with no signposts, and that is to use a compass.

A professor[1] spoke once at a meeting of lecturers and teachers which I attended in the north of France. Instead of discussing the serious difficulties which the country was going through, not least in education, he chose to talk about finding direction. "I want to tell you about the most precious discovery I have made in life," he said. "I used to teach by day and then study by night, not to get a better job but to try and find this precious thing whose name I didn't even know then, but which is called 'inner direction'."

He went on, "A compass has a needle which always points

in the same direction, whichever way you turn the compass, wherever you put it, even if you throw it away... This image is relevant to us, because in every living person there is an inner compass. The moment life begins, the sense of direction awakens."

He quoted Teilhard de Chardin: "On the plane of animate particles, we find the fundamental technique of *groping*, the specific and invincible weapon of all expanding multitudes. This groping strangely combines the blind fantasy of large numbers with the precise orientation of a specific target. It would be a mistake to see it as mere chance. Groping is *directed chance*."[2]

"In man," the professor continued, "this groping is transformed into conscience — which means that the sense of direction becomes conscious and allows man to choose in complete freedom the road he wants to follow."

When I started using this inner compass to explore the area of women's liberation, it was an exhilarating and hopeful experience, giving me the impression of a sort of general upheaval of the cardinal points in the landscape.

It made me wonder if we could start by forgetting ourselves and our struggle for a feminine identity, and decide instead what we want to be free *for* — a goal which would have nothing to do with ourselves and our limitations, and everything to do with the contradictions in the world we live in. Could we decide to become free to create a society where no one is afraid, no one hates, no one grabs what they want — where no one wants to grab because life makes sense and people live with satisfied hearts?

If we want to be liberated *for* that, the list of what we want to be liberated *from* becomes rather different. We need to be liberated from demand, from jealousy, from the passion for pleasure or power, comfort or control. We need to lose our fears, our bitterness, our wish for self-justification, our binding habits, our prejudices. We need to become liberated personalities.

We can demand rights as well. But then this list, too, gets stood on its head. We need the right to be hurt without hurting back, the right to serve, to work hard, to expect no reward, the right to look truth in the face without the padding of lies, the right to give gladly, to sacrifice, and the right to the purity that cleans the body social like a great flow of rich red blood.

My list of rights could easily be mistaken for a list of duties. Yet nothing could be more wrong. If these qualities were imposed on us from outside, they could turn into duties. But personal discovery of them, by following the inner compass, reveals that in fact they are absolutely fundamental rights. They are the key to, and the fruit of, true liberation. And this is the liberation which I want to investigate.

Notes
[1] Theophil Spoerri, Professor of Romance Literature, Rector of Zurich University 1948-50.
[2] Pierre Teilhard de Chardin: *The Phenomenon of Man*, trans. Bernard Wall, Collins, 1965, p. 110.

2

Modern Superstitions

An exploration of this deeper liberation must begin with a study of some of the obstacles to its discovery.

One of the largest of these obstacles — and one powerful enough to make the sturdiest compass needle quiver — could be called superstition. We might think that in so enlightened an age, we have left superstition behind. Not so. There is a new sort — scientific superstition. This phenomenon is already nearly a century old, but only today is it bearing its most bitter fruit, making us believe without evidence or proof a whole series of anti-truths, simply because they are dressed up in apparent scientific authority.

The most disastrous of these anti-truths, and perhaps the most insidious, seems to me to be this: that anything which cannot be measured in terms of scientific instruments or statistics has no objective reality and is therefore not valid. We have come a long way from Pascal, a true scientist, for whom spiritual realities existed beside mathematical realities. "We must know," he writes, "when to doubt, when to feel certain and when to submit. Anyone who does otherwise does not understand the power of reason. There are some who break these rules, either by assuring us that everything can be proved because they understand nothing about the nature of proof; or by doubting everything because they do not know when it is necessary to submit; or by submitting in everything because they do not know when we must use our judgement."[1]

This conflict of views is embodied in the total and often amusing contrast presented by my two grandmothers.

My maternal grandmother, whom we affectionately called by the English name "Granny" although she was Parisian to her finger-tips, had been brought up in a convent. Her overflowing imagination accorded badly with the narrow-mindedness she found there. "You're an instrument of Satan," the Sisters would reply when she asked embarrassing questions. She had been told that in hell a huge clock kept repeating from age to age, in rhythm with its pendulum, "Ever, never, ever, never. . ." This clock used to give her shivers by day and nightmares at night. At the age of fifteen she sent religion packing. She had a church wedding so as not to offend her parents, but she and my grandfather agreed that they would give their children no religious instruction. And they kept to their decision. But when she was fifty, she started to take an interest in spiritualism — the power of positive thought, conversations with the other world, invisible forces — a strange angle from which she imperceptibly came back to her childhood faith, stripped now of the superstitions which had stifled it.

She watched with interest the discovery of faith which I was making myself in those years. During the last years of her life, whenever I visited her, she would wait until we were alone, sit me down at her feet, look me straight in the eyes, and ask:

"Well, my dear, tell me. Do you still believe?"

"Yes, Granny, more than ever."

"Ah," she would say, and she would look more at peace.

She fell ill while I was away. I found her almost unconscious, but she was expecting me for the last time. She pressed my hand and I knew that she had recognised me. Three nights later, I was at her side when her heart, so warm and generous, ceased to beat. Her long struggle with doubt was over.

Grandmaman, on the other hand, was a free-thinker, the embodiment of the university tradition. Her father had been a scientist. For her, human intelligence represented the supreme authority, and stupidity the unpardonable crime. Religion? Mumbo-jumbo! It was one of her favourite expressions. Whenever my sister and I lunched with her, after the meal she would serve us coffee which deserved its fame and accompany it, like a ritual, with an anti-religious tirade lasting ten minutes. Her conscience at peace, she would then send us off to complete our regular Thursday afternoon outing. When my cousin was confirmed, Grandmaman is said to have installed herself right under the pulpit and ostentatiously read a volume of Voltaire throughout the whole ceremony.

She had adopted as an emblem a goat with the motto: "Pede velox, cornu ferox."[2] She had about her a severity, a pugnacity, a tenacity of opinion that I admired. At her funeral the parson seemed to applaud the spirit of this unbeliever, for he chose a text from Revelations: "Would you were either cold or hot!"[3]

And so, from two different angles, I have inherited a certain care for truth: the truth that is thirst for love and the truth that is humility in the face of facts. Both claim an absolute, both live in the light, both reject the half-light of compromise. Never have these two aspects of truth seemed to me contradictory.

The other day I was watching a television programme on medicine and faith-healing. A doctor who had decided to become a minister had been told by a colleague, "This is where our ways part; you take the way of faith, I'll take the way of facts." This sort of remark strikes me as the height of illogicality. Inert matter, energy, living beings, the spirit, all are facts. Each obeys its own laws in its own sphere. I have never understood why the spirit should contradict biology any more than energy contradicts matter.

During the lifetime of my two grandmothers, a silent revolution took place. When they were born, the priest was still the oracle of society. By the time they died, the scientist had replaced him as the trustee of infallibility. The black cassock had given way to the white overall. But are the human hearts that beat under these garments so different? There are always arrogant minds which pose as sole possessors of truth. And there are other minds conscious of their own limits, humble enough to know that truth can never be possessed, only served.

The church has long been accused, sometimes with reason, of favouring superstition. But today one may legitimately begin to wonder if some scientists do not favour moral illiteracy. Some aspects of "science" have burdened us with as much superstition as did the church in medieval times. Those who take it on themselves to ask awkward questions are no longer excommunicated, but they are effectively relegated to outer darkness. They are not heretics, they are out-of-date. And that insult goes deep.

In three spheres which directly affect the life of women — physiology, psychology and sociology — this modern superstition exercises convergent and effective pressures. The result is a kind of back-cloth to our minds, somewhat vague but ever-present, which influences all our judgements. We finish by believing, we are not sure why, that the individual is inevitably conditioned by his molecules, by his subconscious, and by his socio-economic situation. The liberation which is offered us becomes, in fact, a triple slavery. And this has distinctly altered the whole movement for the emancipation of women. So I would like to look more closely at these pressures, the first originating with the materialist biologists, the second with Freud and his disciples, and the third arising from our sociological environment.

Notes
[1] Blaise Pascal: *Pensées*, trans. Martin Turnell, Harvill Press, 1962, No. 355.
[2] "Fleet of foot, fierce of horn."
[3] Revelations 3, 15 (Moffatt's translation).

3

Beast or Beauty

Cambridge is a good place in which to tackle the first of these issues. It was here that Charles Darwin's interest in natural history was aroused, which led him to the discoveries embodied in *Origin of Species*. His family's picturesque house is today the heart of a college bearing his name. Professor Louis Leakey, the anthropologist and archaeologist, taught in Cambridge. His discoveries in the Olduvai Valley in Tanzania made it possible to date the known origin of mankind a million years earlier than had been thought; and he has left an indelible imprint on generations of students and research workers here. It was here too that Crick and Watson penetrated the mystery of the molecular constitution of deoxyribonucleic acid — DNA — and unravelled the working of the genetic code, discoveries which earned them the Nobel Prize.

In Madingley, a charming little village near by, lies hidden an Institute of Animal Behaviour. Two of our friends were working there when we first settled in Cambridge. He was a specialist on chimpanzees; she was studying the effects of weaning and separation from the mother in a group of rhesus monkeys. Once a year the Institute opens its doors to friends and to the curious, so that the experiments going on can be examined at leisure.

I was fascinated by the research on chicks. It is well-known that many birds adopt as their "mother" the first object they see on emerging from the egg. Under normal conditions it is in fact their mother. Here in the laboratory, on the other hand, the emerging chicks were confronted with different things: for example, with colours. One chick then took red for its mother, another blue, and their subsequent reactions to these colours were studied.

Another experiment was conducted on the weaver-bird, which builds its nest by sewing leaves together with grass. A zoologist at Madingley wanted to find out whether it learns to build its nest like that or whether it builds entirely by instinct. He bred fourteen successive generations of weaver-birds which were provided with neither leaves nor grass; they laid their eggs in prefabricated nests. The fifteenth generation at nesting time was given leaves and grass. The bird immediately built a perfect nest, completely typical of its species.

Behaviour patterns are, therefore, indelibly engraved in animal instinct. And if for any reason this instinctive programming is interrupted or deflected, the creature loses its bearings. There was the famous jackdaw who decided that the ethnologist Konrad Lorenz was her fiancé, and when that patient man could not bring himself to accept her ritual offering of a worm placed in his mouth, tried to put it in his ear, but after that found herself totally baffled.

Among the more advanced mammals, in particular among large anthropoid apes, instinct is partly replaced by learning. Gibbons, for example, have regular schools for their young.

Man, who belongs to the animal category, also has a formidable heritage of capabilities, instincts and gifts, which are engraved in the fibres of his being — quite literally, since they are found in every chromosome of each cell. Yet he is not programmed to respond with a set instinctive behaviour pattern to the varied modifications of his existence. But while this faculty is lacking, others, uniquely human, take its place.

One of the principal brain specialists in France is Professor Paul Chauchard. The first time I met him he was Director of the École pratique des Hautes Études at the Sorbonne. To reach him, you climbed numerous staircases and arrived under the eaves, followed a passage around many awkward corners, passed a refrigerator whose contents the uninitiate had best not try to imagine, and there was the professor in a little room, half laboratory and half office, as modest as himself. Since that first meeting, I have listened to many of his lectures. In one which he gave in 1966, he summarised the most recent discoveries about the structure of the human brain:

"Man has often been defined as being three-tiered: the body with its instincts, the reflective intelligence, and the free, responsible being. This highest level is often envisaged as purely spiritual. But that is an error. We now know that the human brain is constructed in three levels which correspond to these three tiers. There is the lower, primitive brain, which controls our unity as an organism and our elementary instincts and emotions; there is a higher, intelligent brain, a machine for feeling, thinking and acting, which also contains acquired reactions; and then there is the prefrontal brain, whose nervous system allows us to stand back from a particular action and consider it, and choose freely a line of conduct which draws on our past experience and which is guided by the desire to shape the future according to an ideal."

He explained that in humans the lower brain is reduced in function, leaving us without the sure guide which animals are given by their instincts. "The satisfaction of human needs depends on the activity of the intelligent brain: we have to move from instinct to knowledge, and from there to habits of action. But to stop at this can itself be a bad habit. Humans have a need not only to learn, but to learn what is good and right, and what is bad and evil. Since our third brain enables us to reflect, we must use it if we want to remain human."

This means that human beings have special capacities, arising from our brain structure, of which the principal one is freedom of choice. The determinism of our heredity is counterbalanced by the freedom inherent in the very construction of our brain. Each one of us is like an artist who is given a palette of paints, with perhaps more of some colours and fewer of others, but who is free to use this range to paint a mess or a masterpiece. *Homo erectus*, the man-ape, has become *homo sapiens* through the exercise of this choice.

The choices which women make in this context affect the future evolution of the human race. There is an old saying, "Educate a man and you educate an individual, educate a woman and you educate a people." Professor Jacob Bronowski in his television series *The Ascent of Man* talked about woman's part in this ascent, by her choice of partner, and by passing on to her children, as she brings them up, the inherited wisdom of mankind, which is no longer instinctive but has to be learnt.

But what should be the basis of our choices? How do you decide, for instance, whom to marry? I once saw a cartoon in which a girl was saying to a young man, "Of course, Tony, I adore you, but I really can't marry all the men I love!" Should the decision be based only on feelings, or are there other considerations? And if your marriage runs into difficulties, are you actually free to *choose* whether it will eventually succeed or not? Professor Chauchard again: "There is often a struggle between the man, acting primarily on reason, and the woman, who puts feelings first. Neurophysiology has now shown clearly that the basic feelings arise from the primitive brain, and cold heartless reason from the intelligent brain. In both cases the dimension is incomplete. A human being is only complete through the use of the prefrontal brain, which coordinates both emotion and reason on a higher level which is the real heart, the real love which surpasses reason without denying it."

Choices taken on so high and so demanding a level might seem to ask too much of us. But the easy way out for us risks becoming the back door for the human race to escape again into the animal world.

Coventry Patmore wrote:
> Ah, wasteful woman, she who may
>   On her sweet self set her own price,
> Knowing man cannot choose but pay,
>   How has she cheapen'd paradise;
> How given for nought her priceless gift,
>   How spoil'd the bread and spill'd the wine,
> Which, spent with due, respective thrift,
>   Had made brutes men, and men divine.[1]

This seems to me to contain not a reproof but a challenge. *Homo erectus, homo sapiens* — and what will we choose next? *Homo extinctus* or *homo sanctus*? Since the atom bomb first made its appearance, we have known that this choice may be decisive not for our distant descendants but for our own children.

Note
[1] Coventry Patmore: 'The Angel in the House' from *Poems*, O.U. Press, 1949, p. 79.

4

Fragments of Freud

For an adequate inquiry into the great schools of classical psychology, Central Europe would be a better place to go than Cambridge. Perhaps due to the Germanic taste for studying the depths of the psyche, many of the theories which have had the greatest impact have been born in Vienna, Switzerland and Germany. Or else there is America, where a record number of psychiatrists, psychologists and psycho-analysts, heirs to the great masters, are practising.

But since our interest is to investigate not psychology itself but its pressure on our everyday life — fragmented, diluted and made available en masse to every last woman in the West — the most useful place to go is perhaps the nearest hairdresser's, where you can settle down quietly in a comfortable chair and stretch out a hand to the pile of women's magazines.

A cartoon: Johnny arrives home bringing his school report, full of zeros. He shows it to his father and asks innocently, "How do you explain that, by heredity or environment?"

A game: "Interpret your own dreams", with a key to the symbols to help you.

A short story: A woman, on the eve of her only son's wedding, is seized with an unreasoning, irresistible impulse and steals a black silk négligé from a shop. The drama unfolds with a series of interrogations of the woman and of her husband, first by the solicitor, then by the psychiatrist.

We are up to our eyes in psycho-analysis.

Whether we like it or not, the very atmosphere we breathe is permeated by the discoveries of our century in this sphere. Why have they had such a vogue? I have a slight suspicion that some people have taken advantage of them to popularise notions which they find convenient, but which are in fact very far from the truth of these discoveries.

There is, for example, the popular idea that Freud said, "If you don't let someone do what he wants, he will have complexes." To begin with, this is a confusion of ideas, since the father of the complex is not Freud, but Adler, who explained the human psyche in terms of the desire for power. What Freud actually said, and what constitutes the heart of his brilliant discoveries, is that no living impulse of the human psyche can be cancelled out. It will be either expressed in action, or sublimated into a higher impulse, or forced back into the subconscious and there, far from disappearing, will reappear in a thousand inescapable behaviour patterns. It will continue its underground work until it is again brought into the light of the conscious, and is cured by that light.

It is therefore untrue to say that the word "no" does not exist in Freud's vocabulary. On the contrary, the "no" is indispensable beside the "yes"; the principle of law beside that of pleasure; the father, the embodiment of the former, beside the mother, the embodiment of the latter.

The second false concept can be summed up in the phrase, "It's not my fault, it's my subconscious." This is all the more beguiling in that it contains a grain of truth. We are in fact conditioned by reactions deeply buried since infancy, whether or not we accept the strongly sexual flavour that Freud gives them. From that point to the denial of responsibility for our subconscious is a step easily taken, because it is a very convenient form of excuse. But is it true?

Without rushing off to the psycho-analyst, we can find within ourselves, as well as the inner compass, a sort of precious inner lighthouse. There is the experience which many people have and which is a gift of grace, of remembering an event long forgotten but which has been decisive for the whole of our lives. When it suddenly comes to the surface again, it is vital to seize the chance, to accept the pain which comes with the light of clarity, and to untie what has become knotted up.

A woman I know had experienced terrible tragedy in her family, and a particularly painful incident in her childhood had caused her to close her heart resolutely towards one relative. Fifteen years later, the incident came back to her mind. She struggled against the clarity that came with remembrance: "I was much too young! It wasn't my fault!" But at that moment the thought came to her, "If you were mature enough to close your heart, you were mature enough to open it." She stopped hiding behind excuses, accepted total responsibility for what she herself had done, and on that basis was able to build a completely new relationship with that member of her family.

Sometimes it is not a memory which brings the light but an act of our own which surprises us, or someone else's remark. St Paul says that this inner light is able "to turn the thing it shines upon into light also".[1] This is the light which can liberate us, instantly or gradually, from the grip of the subconscious.

There has been controversy for many years about the scientific status of the theories of the great psychologists. The modern mind asks for experiments, proofs, statistics. But when it is a question of human beings, it is not easy to agree on what is meant by "scientific". Can the study of the human psyche really be reduced to neuro-physiology and behavioural statistics? Do these two disciplines really encompass the whole of man? If not, is reliance on them not directly against the very principles of the experimental method, which demand that the experiment should be perfectly adapted to its object?

I once read about an experiment carried out in California. Five hundred spectators in a cinema had been attached to electrodes linked to a recording instrument, and then shown a pornographic film. The conclusion of the experiment — according to the instrument — was that pornography has absolutely no effect on the human being. Pornography merchants and police commissioners would have needed no instrument and would have provided a much more accurate result.

In America, too, questionnaires have been worked out for the study of personality, very full questionnaires which the subject himself has to answer. The University of Minnesota's Personality Inventory, for instance, consists of 550 questions. But it has to provide in addition for controls which evaluate the lie factor, the confusion factor, and the factor of subconscious refusal to face the questions asked.

Anyway, even if an accurate mean of current human behaviour were established, what would it signify? In a species in evolution, are not the exceptional individuals, the mutants, often the truest representatives of that evolution?

Professor Pierre Debray-Ritzen, who certainly cannot be accused of spirituality, writes in *La Scolastique freudienne*: "Each of us is unique in genes and unique in spirit, that is to say in the unique arrangement, from the earliest months of existence, of millions of brain circuits. Hence our 'deepest being', which it seems ridiculous to want to categorise..."[2]

There is one paragraph of Freud which is rather unexpected for anyone who has only glanced at the surface of his thought: "We believe that civilisation has been built up by sacrifices in gratification of the primitive impulses, and that it is to a great extent for ever being recreated as each individual repeats the sacrifice of his instinctive pleasures for the common good. The sexual are amongst the most important of the instinctive forces thus utilised: they are in this way sublimated, that is to say, their energy is turned aside from its sexual goal and diverted towards other ends, no longer sexual and socially more valuable."[3]

J.D. Unwin quotes this paragraph in his book *Sex and Culture*. Unwin is a rationalist who offers no moral or value judgements on the results of his research. "We cannot bask in the sunshine of theory before we have plunged into the cold waters of fact," he writes.[4] And he provides facts in plenty. He studied the sexual customs and the levels of culture reached by eighty primitive societies, and observed an exact parallel between the degree of restriction of sexual practices and the cultural level attained by these societies.

"There were very few uncivilised societies who compelled a girl to confine her sexual activity to one man throughout her life... I do not know of a single case in which a man was compelled to limit his sexual qualities to one woman; this custom has been in force only in some civilised societies. Those societies which have maintained the custom for the longest period have attained the highest position in the cultural scale which the human race has yet reached."[5]

Unwin then tried to determine whether these parallels between chastity and the level of social energy represented cause and effect. He came to the conclusion, after studying Freud and other psychologists, that they did:

"Every human society possesses potential social energy; the ability to adapt thought and reason to the details of the inherited tradition is inherent in the human organism; but a display of that energy, the psychologists assert, depends upon sacrifices in the gratification of innate desires, the energy arising from the emotional conflict producing a depth of thought and enterprise which is not manifest except under those conditions."[6]

This is an important point for our time, when territorial conquest is forbidden in face of the risk of atomic destruction, and when our energies could be channelled instead into a real growth in the spirit of service and solidarity.

The Austrian psychologist Viktor Frankl estimates that, after explaining 80 per cent of psychological troubles by the various traditional theories, there remains 20 per cent entirely due to what he calls "existential frustration" — what you and I express in the phrase, "Life has no meaning." His cure, which he calls logotherapy, consists in helping the individual to recover a sense of purpose.

Frankl's thought was formed in the hottest of crucibles — a concentration camp. He wrote after this experience:

"Everything can be taken from a man but one thing: the last of the human freedoms — to choose one's attitude in any given set of circumstances, to choose one's own way.

"And there were always choices to make. Every day, every hour, offered the opportunity to make a decision, a decision which determined whether you would or would not submit to those powers which threatened to rob you of your very self, your inner freedom; which determined whether or not you would become the plaything of circumstance, renouncing freedom and dignity to become moulded into the form of the typical inmate."[7]

There is a new perspective. A purpose in life: perhaps that is the key. If the purpose is high enough, if it is pursued with enough passion and discipline, it can take along in its slipstream the subconscious itself, creating in the end an integrated and harmonious personality, and bringing inner liberation with it.

Notes
[1] Ephesians 5, 8 (J.B. Phillips' translation).
[2] Pierre Debray-Ritzen: *La Scolastique freudienne*, Fayard, 1972, p. 82.
[3] Sigmund Freud: *Introductory Lectures on Psycho-Analysis*, tr. J. Rivière, London, 1928, p. 17; quoted by J.D. Unwin: *Sex and Culture*, O.U. Press, 1934, p. 314.
[4] J.D. Unwin, op. cit., p. 2.
[5] Ibid, pp. 24-5.
[6] Ibid, p. 317.
[7] Viktor E. Frankl: *Man's Search for Meaning: An Introduction to Logotherapy*, tr. Ilse Lasch, Hodder and Stoughton, 1964, pp. 66-7, 65-6.

5

Fantastic

Let anyone who likes swallow the pill. I prefer not to swallow fantasies. And on the subject of contraception, we are being asked to swallow a few sizeable ones.

Pressured by threats of overpopulation and famine, by statistics, by socio-scientific arguments from all angles, it is difficult to keep one's own inner freedom of choice, and the compass can seem irrelevant. But these sociological pressures are as much an obstacle as those arising from physiological or psychological thought, and have to be looked at as clearly.

Ten years ago, in Paris, I was having coffee with five or six women. There was much talk of the new legislation going through the Assembly, which was to rescind the 1920 law forbidding abortion. A doctor's wife was passionately for it. "Naturally," she said, "I exclude the unmarried." Sitting on one side of her was a young girl, and on the other an older single woman. Intrigued, I asked how she intended to "exclude" her neighbours. She waved my question away and continued her argument. An article in Le Monde[1] developed the same theme: "In any case, at the moment the family planning movement is not demanding the free sale of contraceptives to young people but only, on medical advice, to married couples."

And that was the first fantasy. We were asked to believe that, once the principle of contraception had been accepted for extreme cases, the demand would stop of its own accord at a reasonable point. The facts of human nature already showed clearly that it would do nothing of the sort. In the same year I talked to the warden of a hostel for women students in Paris, where one of the girls was studying medicine. Her fellow students were constantly asking her for contraceptives, and she had the greatest difficulty in defending the gates these determined young women were trying to force. A less scrupulous person would have made a tidy little income out of it.

A short eight years exploded that fantasy. In 1974, without fuss, a law was passed in France authorising family planning centres to give contraceptives, without charge and without consulting parents, to girls of thirteen to eighteen.

Another fantasy, which in the course of the same ten years has assumed vast proportions, is that contraception offers an alternative to abortion. When the campaign in favour of contraception got into full swing, the main purpose, apparently, was to produce a remedy to the disastrous practice of back-street abortion. The reasoning appeared simple and logical: back-street abortion is an intolerable horror; legalise contraception and you will have abolished it.

What has happened in reality? After ten years of more and more liberal use of contraceptives, a vociferous campaign has been launched to obtain the right to free abortion. I shall never forget a Saturday morning in the market square of my town when a group of young students, painted to make a redskin in war regalia pale with envy, mobbed the housewives to get them to sign a petition demanding the right to abortion on social security. And don't forget that those girls already had completely free access to all contraceptives.

I have always been intrigued by the way Christians, and particularly Christian women, seem to swallow these fantasies. Once, on a visit to a town in eastern France, I was given hospitality by a woman who had taken considerable social responsibility in her parish and beyond. At breakfast one morning she started to talk about the pill: a certain number of young and not-so-young women, active in the Protestant church, were campaigning for family planning. When I expressed slight surprise at this double commitment, she was astonished at my surprise, and the conversation continued something like this:

I: "I can understand it perfectly well when social workers and doctors, faced with possible tragedies, prescribe the pill as a lesser evil — an emergency measure, if you like. But it seems to me that the church should be concerned rather with the long-term solution, with the promise that God is more powerful than physical appetite or human selfishness."

She: "All the same, you can't hope that the majority of mankind will accept that sort of solution?"

I: "I don't know, but I do know that it's very important that the star of purity which lights man's road doesn't die. The 'majority of mankind' hasn't landed on the moon either, but when only two astronauts did it the headlines said, 'Man Conquers the Moon'. And I think they were right — what one person achieves, everyone else potentially can do too."

She: "But that's for saints! It's Utopia!"

I: "I think it's only a question of one or two per cent of the ordinary people showing by the way we live that purity is more satisfying than promiscuity. And it seems to me normal to expect to find this one or two per cent in the ranks of the churches. Don't the churches say that the Creator of all instincts is the best master of those instincts?"

She: "If you believe that, you *must* have faith!"

But what about her basic question? Can we hope that the majority of mankind will accept a solution based on mutual respect of the sexes? It is tempting to answer in the negative. But two French doctors, François and Michèle Guy, have written a book which proposes a different answer. They spent some years working in the poorer areas of the island of Mauritius, which cannot be said to represent a favoured élite — the population increase there was one of the highest in the world. They based their work entirely on the education of married couples, and they aimed especially to give fathers a sense of their responsibilities. The resulting improvements were striking. Over four years the rate of population increase fell from 30.3 to 21.9 per cent, in spite of a rise in the number of fertile women.[2]

There is an overpopulation problem; it would be stupid to adopt an ostrich attitude towards it. But it appears to me essential that, faced with such a problem, we should at least think a little before rushing into solutions that are perhaps no solutions at all, and above all before advocating them for others, let alone imposing them.

The West's solution for the moment is to dissociate sexual pleasure as completely as possible from the act of creation.

Promiscuity is encouraged, procreation discouraged. Could this be another fantasy? Despite the most resounding declarations on responsible parenthood, the message actually being transmitted to future generations is quite different: Do what you like — the only thing that matters is to avoid the consequences. This attitude is becoming more and more widespread and represents the very essence of irresponsibility.

This fantasy world also conceals a subtle hypocrisy — a vice of which we accuse the 19th century and the middle classes, imagining that by our own free speaking we have freed ourselves of it. But is it not hypocritical to condemn a dictator for getting rid of people who inconvenience him, when we ourselves do not hesitate to get rid of unborn people who might possibly inconvenience us?

Margaret White, who is both magistrate and doctor, wrote an article in *The Times* which concluded with these words: "In a civilised, caring society, no one should be unwanted, however inadequate or handicapped. Yet in Britain today being unwanted is the only crime punishable by death, and the unborn child has no right of appeal."[3]

Could it be possible that the way out of this dilemma is to reconsider the purpose and use of sexual energy? Freud and Unwin, as I have already quoted them, both equate personal sacrifice with social creativity. They seem to look on discipline as an accelerator, not a brake. A contemporary Indian journalist takes the same view. Rajmohan Gandhi, grandson of the Mahatma, writes:

"I do not agree with all that the Mahatma said or urged. . . I am with him in his belief that husband and wife could live together and love each other without necessarily going into bed with each other when they pleased. . .

"A massive movement of and for purity would have three effects:

1. It would naturally control the growth of population.

2. It would increase affection of people for one another inside and outside the family.

3. It would enable men and women to work harder and produce more. . .

"I can wager that our women and our men in village or city

will comprehend the concept of purity far more quickly than they grasp the loop or sterilisation. And they will be far more satisfied with it."[4]

So to fantasy there is an alternative. Genesis tells the story of the fantasy which Eve was the first to listen to. But the Genesis story ends with the promise that the woman will one day crush the serpent's head.

Notes
[1] *Le Monde*, 13 April 1966.
[2] François and Michèle Guy: *Île Maurice — Régulation des naissances et action familiale*, Mappus, Lyon, 1968.
[3] *The Times*, 21 July 1975.
[4] *Himmat*, Bombay, 14 April 1967.

6

Secret Classroom

Sociological pressures begin early and are inescapable. One day we were playing the game in which one child in each team has to draw a picture representing a word, and get his team to guess what the word is. The word was "family". In one team, the child drew, crude but recognisable, a father, a mother and a child, and after a few seconds someone shouted, "Family!" In another team, the three characters all looked alike. The children made all sorts of guesses: a class, a regiment, a bus queue. No one could get it right. Suddenly the artist had the idea of adding a television set, and immediately the face of one of his team lit up: "A family!"

This small incident pinpointed for me how deeply the mass media have penetrated the intimacy of our lives. In America, it is estimated that a pupil at the end of secondary education will have spent an average of 6,800 hours at school, and more than 20,000 hours in front of the television. Television, press, radio and cinema could be called "the secret classroom". The child learns about life and the world at least as much through the media as through school. And while the teacher's capacity and right to teach are proved by examinations and diplomas, no proof is demanded of those who reach the public through the microphone or the small screen.

Like all human inventions — like printing in its time — mass communications represent a formidable potential for good or for evil. In themselves they are neutral, but they become instruments of progress or decadence according to the way they are used. The media have so direct and deep an influence on our children that they are of vital interest to all women.

If a butcher sells bad meat or a baker mouldy bread, there

is a way of protecting our families: there are laboratories which can test whether food is fresh or harmful, and there are laws and penalties. We do not have the same protection against comics, radio and television. And society seems to have given up a basic consensus on standards, on what is tolerable and what is not. The result is that the media have become a free-for-all which you may deplore, but which, if you are realistic, you cannot ignore.

All sorts of emotional currents complicate the situation. Take the words "censorship" and "propaganda". They are guaranteed to raise the hackles of the most placid. Everyone who loves freedom has a deep instinctive reaction against censorship — and it is right and proper that this should be so. Creativity can only flourish in a climate of freedom. But in all areas of human activity there exists a sort of internal law of survival which produces an indispensable "self-censorship". There are certain limits beyond which culture risks destroying itself. We may oppose the idea of delegating to one person the power to fix these limits, but it is contrary to common sense to maintain that the limits do not exist.

With the word "propaganda" we reach the heart of the subject, but we also land in the midst of ambiguity. In fact, there is no life without propaganda; everything living has a message which it propagates. The dog wags its tail, the child hops down the street kicking a stone, in a spontaneous kind of propaganda for the delight of being alive. My choices, my likes and dislikes, my enthusiasms and rejections, my integrity and compromises, all affect the people near me and influence them through their imitation or their reaction. The Renaissance was, in some ways, nothing more than the spontaneous propaganda of free minds in favour of an idea that they considered superior.

But there are different levels of propaganda, and it is important to know and recognise them. One level is connected with the human desire for security. If we start doing something we are not sure we should be doing, we do not rest until other people are doing it too. The man with a drink problem is never secure until he has put a glass in the hand of each of his companions. This form of propaganda also depends on a stubborn illusion, common to most mortals, that if others were more like us the world would be considerably improved.

This has an important bearing on women's liberation. Indeed there is a branch of the movement which has completely abandoned objectivity. Women who have had one or more terminations of pregnancy unite, publish a manifesto and become ardent advocates of abortion. Lesbians become absolutely determined to impose their point of view on all other women. This shows up on every page of magazines like *Spare Rib* in England and *Ms* in America. Thus fascist-type mini-dictatorships are formed, all the more pernicious in that they refuse to recognise themselves as propaganda. I say "fascist-type" deliberately, for is not the essence of fascism summed up in the phrase, "I am right, so I have the right to power"?

We need to have our eyes open. When a new idea appears, it is good to ask if it is in fact a new idea, or an old one being pushed by a person or a group of people trying to justify themselves by dragging others along with them. One area in which women seem particularly vulnerable is fashion. It matters little if a fashion is set by prostitutes or Lesbians — we eagerly fall into step. Yet if there is one area in which mini-dictatorships function, it is this, and the coalition of models, fashion houses and the women's press represents a formidable alliance.

Another level of propaganda is the conscious manipulation of the mass media for financial or political ends. In a liberal society this kind of propaganda, when it is really blatant, has little effect. During the Occupation, if we happened to listen to Radio Paris, we always had at the back of our minds the jingle:

> "Radio-Paris ment,
> Radio-Paris ment,
> Radio-Paris est allemand."[1]

There are some countries, of course, where propaganda has been elevated into an exact science and where it is almost impossible to escape its grip. The extraordinary demonstrations there in recent years of the resistance of free spirits to the most massive propaganda holds an urgent lesson for all of us.

But the manipulation of propaganda is usually more subtle and even Machiavellian. Betty Friedan's book *The Feminine Mystique* contains a haunting chapter on publicity. It deals with a market study ordered by a company producing electrical household equipment, which showed that the best customer — at any rate, the most vulnerable — is the woman who stays at home dissatisfied. So when the company advertises in a women's magazine, it makes sure that the stories in it support the ideal of the woman in the home, but from an angle which makes this ideal unattainable in practice. Women barred from a career and bored with housework then rush off to the shops like sheep to buy things they do not need.[2] Advertising has its legitimate function of giving information; but lack of purpose makes us its dupes.

Of all the media, to my mind theatre is one of the most creative, the one in which the intentions and influence of the originator are clearest. George Bernard Shaw defined theatre as "a factory of thought, a prompter of conscience, an elucidator of social conduct, an armoury against despair and dullness, and a temple of the Ascent of Man".[3] This definition matches the authentic theatre tradition of Greece and of the medieval church. Today not everyone, to put it mildly, would subscribe to it.

The programme note for Sartre's play *Loser Wins* is an indication of where modern taste has gone:

"Here is your pleasant evening — an old man dying of cancer, a madman in hiding, a background of torture and massacre, incest, two suicides, and endless anguish. 'Madmen tell the truth, Werner.' 'Really? What truth?' 'There is only one truth: the horror of being alive.' Sartre offers you the pleasure of this series of unhappy events which are, in fact, beautiful tragedies. You will be brought face to face with the worst — crime without remission, destiny without fruition, remorse without forgiveness, pain without meaning — and at the end you will feel better, you will say thank you, you will applaud. The naked truth of a man, of all men, is like coffee: black, but a tonic."

A cult has also grown of art for art's sake, claiming to

produce works which do not carry any message. One reply to artists who maintain that they are simply reflecting contemporary meaninglessness comes from Joseph Hayes of the *New York Times*: "Might it not be possible that. . . the writers of these acclaimed works are only imposing their own sick views on the public, with the gleeful co-operation of the critics?"[4] In fact, all theatre has a message; like the wagging tail on the dog, it makes its own propaganda.

In Bordeaux, at a performance of *The Passion according to Sade* by Julian Beck's Living Theatre, the audience slashed the scenery, demolished the piano and attacked the author. Delighted, he gave a shout of triumph. He had wanted to provoke a reaction from his audience and he had done it. This incident throws light on another issue. Political power is balanced by an opposition; financial power is balanced by trade unions. Cultural power, however, has become so totalitarian that it is no longer counter-balanced, since even the dislike and hostility of the public can be turned to its advantage. Cultural power is not responsible to anything or anybody. That is perhaps why it so easily follows the permissive downward path.

What is to be done? There remains only one way — that of Hercules in the Augean stables. A powerful river must wash away the whole dung-heap. The silent majority must take the place of Hercules. It is useless to get indignant. It is useless to campaign for censorship and prohibition. It is useless to keep on appealing to decency and common sense. The dung-heap will continue to grow until such time as a great purifying stream wells up from the depth of our consciences and the strength of our convictions, a stream which will demand of writers and actors that they give back to culture its mission and its destiny.

Pope Paul VI, speaking in St. Peter's to personalities in the press, theatre, radio, television and cinema, said: "You are not asked to set yourselves up as systematic moralists; but credit is still given to your magic power to disclose the field of light that lies behind the mystery of human life."[5]

Notes
[1] "Radio Paris is lying, Radio Paris is German."

[2] Betty Friedan: *The Feminine Mystique*, Dell, New York, 1963, pp. 197-223.
[3] George Bernard Shaw: *Our Theatres in the Nineties*, Constable, 1948, p. VII.
[4] Joseph Hayes: 'Distorted Views', *New York Times*, 11 August 1963.
[5] Paul VI: *La Documentation catholique*, Paris, 4 June 1967, p. 1002.

7
Fried Snowball

Simone de Beauvoir once used an expression which has caught on and has become the focus for yet another set of sociological pressures: "One is not born, but rather becomes, a woman."[1] Is this true?

Theories attributing "psychosexual neutrality" to the newborn infant were current during the sixties, but researchers began to change their opinions after 1968, when studies on the biological development of the embryo were more advanced. It is now known that from conception, when sex is determined by the sex chromosomes — XX for females and XY for males — the male and female embryos develop in completely different patterns. From the seventh week, the gonad differs and the hormones produced by the embryo itself come into action, considerably modifying development, including that of the brain.

A well-documented book on this subject, *Gender Differences: Their Ontogeny and Significance*, contains an account by Ivan N. Mensh of the work of the Gender Identity Research Clinic of the University of California at Los Angeles. After studying the different factors of gender identity — genetic, psychological, social and biological — the researchers conclude that "assigned sex, biological sex and gender identity in the normally developing individual are coincident and are established early in life".[2]

The book also contains a chapter by Corinne Hutt, who comes to this conclusion: "From the very early weeks of uterine life, males and females develop in characteristically different ways. . . From the moment of birth onwards differences in structure, in metabolism, in physiological and psychological functions characterise the development of the two sexes. Many of these non-cognitive differences are shared not only with other societies which manifest many different culture patterns. . . but with other primates as well. . . This fact alone makes a purely environmental interpretation of sex differences difficult to countenance. . .

"The fact that such functional dimorphism exists may be unacceptable to many human females, but denial of it does not prove its absence. . . Cultures and societies cannot create differences — they can only reflect and modulate those which already exist."[3]

It was in the year after the publication of this book that Arianna Stassinopoulos entered the debate. She was finishing her studies at Cambridge when we first arrived there, and her presidency of the Cambridge Union had earned her attention beyond the confines of the university. An economist, she went to London the following year to prepare her thesis for a doctorate. There she published her book *The Female Woman*. It is at the same time an erudite, extremely well-documented book, and a polemic work attacking the intellectual arrogance of the women's liberation movement. It is also clearly the work of a contented woman, and this in itself gives the book a remarkable impact. In her second chapter she analyses woman's distinctive, innate characteristics:

"Culturally we are now 'industrial men and women', but genetically we still carry within us the hunters and the child-bearers — our not-so-distant ancestors. We could not possibly have had sufficient time to evolve genetically away from our ancestral model. Men have been hunters for several million years. Settled agriculture has only existed for some thousands of years, and industry about two hundred — mere seconds in evolutionary and geological time.

"It is inconceivable that millions of years of evolutionary selection during a period of a marked sexual division of labour have not left pronounced traces on the innate character of men and women. Aggressiveness, and mechanical and spatial skills, a sense of direction, and physical strength — all masculine characteristics — are the qualities essential for a hunter. . . The prolonged period of dependence of human children, the difficulty of carrying the peculiarly heavy and inert human body — a much heavier, clumsier burden than the monkey infant and much less able to cling on for safety — meant that women could not both look after their children and be hunters and explorers. Early humans learned to take advantage of this period of dependence to transmit rules, knowledge, and skills to their offspring — women needed to develop verbal skills, a talent for personal relationships, and a predilection for nurturing going even beyond the maternal instinct. The survival of the core of these qualities in the form of specifically female innate characteristics can easily be seen in women's everyday behaviour."[4]

So if we cannot help being born women, the real question is: what sort of women do we become? Or to put it another way, which ideology do we choose?

Nikita Khrushchev, when he visited America in 1959, used a characteristically picturesque expression: "Coexistence between ideologies is as unthinkable as fried snowballs." In the West we are not yet very good at understanding what an ideology is — an idea that mobilises the whole of our being, our resources, our passions, our intellect, our will, our action. But on the question of the role of women, there are indeed two ideologies, and they are as incompatible as a snowball and a frying-pan. A few women are consciously committed to one or the other, but we are all, whether we like it or not, oriented towards one or the other. There is no neutral zone. These two ideologies coexist in most of us, but they are at war, and the outcome of the war depends on our daily decisions.

One of these ideologies puts "me" first, the other puts "me" last. The one promises self-realisation, self-expression and self-satisfaction; the other promises nothing at all, except that the seed which dies bears much fruit. The one demands schools, hospitals and houses; the other arouses a sense of vocation in teachers, doctors and nurses, architects. The one claims rights, the other spends itself satisfying needs.

There is an odd fact about the kingdom of "Me first". You might think that so many people devoted to expressing themselves would create an extremely diversified society upon which each would leave the mark of his profound originality.

In fact, it is not like that. The further you look, the more everyone seems alike — so much so that it becomes difficult to distinguish between men and women, and even children seem to be grown-ups in miniature. And if you say to yourself hopefully, "Well, since the sexes are so like each other, they ought to be able to live happily with each other", you are wrong again. It is in the kingdom of "Me first" that the sex war is fiercest.

Paradoxically, it is in the kingdom of "The seed which dies" that the differences are accentuated, each personality revealing its unique qualities, masculine and feminine totally distinct but in fruitful co-operation.

Notes
[1] Simone de Beauvoir: *The Second Sex*, Penguin Books, 1972, p. 296.
[2] Christopher Ounsted and David C. Taylor: *Gender Differences: Their Ontogeny and Significance*, Churchill Livingstone, 1972, p. 52.
[3] Ibid, pp. 112-14.
[4] Arianna Stassinopoulos, *op. cit.*, pp. 37-8.

8

Radical

Obstacles and pressures — we are all aware, to a greater or lesser extent, of their existence, and of their effect on us and on people near us. We would like to get round or through them, and walk the road to liberation. The same is true of our society, faced with immense opportunities but uncertain how to realise them. Solutions which solve nothing are one of the most depressing features of our age. Social remedies either are futile or else turn out to be worse than the disease.

Communism stepped forward as a remedy to dictatorship, and it has bred more dictatorship. Fascism stepped forward as a remedy to the confusion of Communism, but it only succeeded in putting a temporary lid on the seething pot and compounding cruelty and violence. Economic growth, which was to raise the standard of living, in the end has lowered the quality of life by causing pollution and is leaving the poor even poorer than they were. Contraceptives were supposed to lessen the number of unwanted pregnancies, but by encouraging promiscuity they have rather increased them. The list is interminable. The cause of failure is always the same: the remedy does not go to the root of the evil.

Having investigated the obstacles, however, I would now like to propose a bold first step on our journey, and to look at a possible radical solution. What is the root whose fruits are dictatorship, violence, unwanted children, pollution, poverty; and at home, bitterness, cynicism, emptiness and — yes — dictatorship? I believe the root is the unchallenged human heart and will, the selfish motives which we hide from ourselves more successfully than from others. And I believe that our role as women who are responsible for the future is first of all to accept a radical change in our own human character.

We shall only be able to bring a real cure to the needs around us, and to the agonising problems of the hour, if we first of all try to cure our own jealousies and bitternesses, our demand to be right and to be first, our refusal to serve or to suffer. The cure sometimes needs to be drastic.

Queen Victoria was a woman not always easy to live with. As a girl she declared that if, when she got married, her husband opposed her will, it would be "a dreadful thing". And Prince Albert had to wage a battle, in extremely difficult conditions, to alter his wife's character. At the very outset of their marriage he encountered a weakness common in women — our tendency to dominate some people and to submit unduly to others.

When Victoria came to the throne, her first concern was to free herself from her mother's grasp. In fact, her first act as Queen was to state that she would no longer sleep in the same room as her mother. But as so often happens, having rebelled against family authority, she quickly fell under the domination of one of her friends. Baroness Lehzen, with the Prime Minister, Lord Melbourne, and the Paget family, actually managed nearly all the details of her public and her private life. The Baroness was "my beloved, angelic Lehzen". And relations between the Queen and Melbourne were sufficiently doubtful for the crowd to receive the Sovereign one day, when she appeared on her balcony at Ascot, with shouts of "Mrs Melbourne!"

When Prince Albert, at the age of twenty-one, arrived in London for his wedding he found that, although the Queen loved him, he had to tackle this all-powerful clique. They hoped to make short work of the young stranger, and tried to lay down the law to him. They had counted without two fundamental qualities: his determination, and a selflessness which led him to work for the good of the Queen and of the country without any ambition for himself.

Patiently, from month to month, he established his authority, at first within the family circle and then as Prince Consort. The Prime Minister finally included him among his advisers. Baroness Lehzen resented Prince Albert's intervention, and once, when he lost patience and ordered her to leave the Palace, she replied that he had no right to turn her out of the Queen's house. Nevertheless, and by this time with Victoria's help, he succeeded in putting an end to the Baroness's rule over the nursery.

The following year, after the elections, Lord Melbourne disappeared from the scene and the Baroness's power decreased rapidly. A few months later she left England for good. It was only then that Prince Albert told the Queen frankly what he thought of the relationship between the two women. She was horrified: "I blame myself for my blindness. . . . I shudder to think what my beloved Albert had to go through. . . it makes my blood boil to think of it." Freed from the unhealthy influences that had surrounded her, the Queen began to develop her latent qualities — an inner change due to the courage of a man who loved her and was not afraid to stand up to her.[1]

An American friend of mine tells the story of an Englishwoman who came to stay in her parents' home, when she herself was in her rebellious twenties. The Englishwoman was tiny, white-haired, and brimming with a passion for women in their homes to be a force for good in society. She made friends with the girl, and discovered what her life consisted of. Then she went into battle. One day she sat down next to her and asked,

"You're writing a letter?"
"Yes."
"Who to?"
"A boy friend."
"Is he married?"
"Yes."

The woman looked at her. "At home, we have a word for girls who do that," she said, and left.

The girl sat there, shaken to her roots. The woman had reached the reality behind the glamour. The letter was torn up, and was the last of its kind. Later, the American girl married the Englishwoman's son, and they have used their home to bring the same kind of radical change into people's lives.

A wise man I knew once visited a girls' school. He was received by the headmistress, who was very upset that morning; one of her pupils had just been caught stealing. "What are we to do?" the headmistress asked him. "Should she be expelled?"

The man was concerned not so much about the girl, whom he did not know, as about the headmistress, who was a prisoner of her own self-righteousness. He asked her, "When did you steal last?" The headmistress had the humility to remember. In fact, every one of the teachers could remember an incident in the more or less distant past when they had stolen. "Why," said the man cheerfully, "we're nothing but a pack of thieves!" The girl was not expelled and, moved by the honesty of the headmistress and the teachers, she found the courage to make a fresh start. It was a turning point as well in the life of the headmistress, who discovered a new meaning and perspective for education.

There is a price to pay in applying radical solutions; it is a change in our nature. We can accept it or refuse it. There are moments of choice. When a friend offers me a truth about myself, or an enemy throws one full in my face, when I see something amiss under the surface in someone else's life, or begin to feel that things around me are going awry, I have two options. I can either turn my back on the truth and try to go on as before, or look straight at the truth and change. All our human resources of clarity and courage are not enough, you will say. But who is stopping us from appealing to divine resources? And if we are bent on competing with the men, we can always show that we accept change quicker than they!

The road which is opened up by this possibility of radical change is not a theoretical road, but one which leads through the rough and smooth of our daily lives.

Note
[1] Garth Lean: *Brave Men Choose*, Blandford, 1961, pp. 115-21.

9

For Better For Worse

The original recipe for marriage is one of absolute simplicity: a "yes" which commits a man and a woman to a privileged relationship for the whole of the rest of their lives. In some ceremonies, the content of this commitment is made more explicit. After declaring their intention to marry, each partner says to the other, "I take thee. . . to have and to hold from this day forward, for better for worse, for richer for poorer, in sickness and in health, to love and to cherish, till death us do part."

This formula is neither the result of chance nor an artificial fabrication. It has deep roots in three different areas. The first is quite simply the human heart. All lovers in the world want their feelings to be eternal, and poets from the earliest times up to the present have put words to what every person, from the roughest to the most civilised, has at some time felt. Juliet speaks for us all when she begs Romeo:

"O, swear not by the moon, th' inconstant moon,
That monthly changes in her circled orb,
Lest that thy love prove likewise variable."[1]

The second area is the more prosaic one of the legislation in our Western countries, where monogamy is still the rule, even if, bending to the morality of the day, it now tends to authorise successive monogamies.

In the third place, from the point of view of the believer, these phrases represent the highest conception that we have of the divine will for a human couple. Christ said, "No man must separate what God has joined together."[2]

The expression "trial marriage" seems to me a contradiction in terms. I can understand what is meant by trial sex, but marriage contains an element of permanence which excludes the idea of trial. This permanence is then reflected in sexual life in terms of stability, trust and lack of haste.

Seen from this point of view, marriage is clearly a commitment and not a feeling, even if feeling plays a very important part. From his prison cell Dietrich Bonhoeffer wrote a sermon for the wedding of one of his nieces, in which he made an interesting comment on the relationship between love and marriage:

"Just as it is the crown, and not merely the will to rule, that makes the king, so it is the marriage, and not merely your love for each other, that joins you together in the sight of God and man. . . It is not your love that sustains marriage, but from now on, the marriage that sustains your love."[3]

Being realistic is a help. Married love is like a stream that freshens and brightens the countryside; if it stops flowing, it is usually because there is a blockage. It may be something apparently trivial, but that does not make the blockage less effective. One day I spent more than I should have on a kitchen utensil. It was not an extravagant amount, but our budget was very tight and I ought not to have given in. I made a plan to save money on other things, but I did not tell my husband what I had done. Suddenly there was a wall between us. In the few seconds it took me to tell him the exact amount I had spent, the wall vanished. We have often experienced the almost magical effect of these moments of honesty, about a temptation, a mistake, a disappointment, a fear, a hope. Love needs truth to remain alive, and nothing stifles it more than the desperate efforts of our pride to present a better image of ourselves than the reality.

Often, of course, the division is more serious. One fine day an unsuspected weakness is discovered, and a weakness which deeply hurts. A hard-working, conscientious man suddenly realises that his wife is extravagant and has run up debts. A woman who treasures courage above all other virtues finds that her husband has a streak of cowardice. A naturally jealous wife discovers her husband flirting.

Michel Quoist, in his book *The Christian Response*, offers sane advice: "If you're still married to your dream, you're acting like an adolescent. Blame only yourself for your folly and stop blaming your husband or wife for not living up to your ideal. . . It's never too late to really 'marry' the one who shares bed and board with you. You have only to make up your mind to do it. Three is a crowd: your wife, yourself, and your dream. If you really want to get married, divorce your dream."[4]

Of course, if you think about it even a little, it is obvious how completely unreasonable it is to reproach the other person for not conforming to your dreams. You did not marry a dream, you married a human being, filled with good qualities and with shortcomings; and if, in the wonder — and perhaps in the selfishness — of your first love, you were not able to see clearly, it is quite unfair to blame the other person. But in this situation we are rarely reasonable. It touches so intimately the deepest fibres of our being, it destroys so completely the ambitions and hopes of a lifetime, that it feels intolerable. And at that moment the temptation to run away raises its head, in every guise ranging from resignation to divorce to suicide.

There is a total contrast between the public image of these "solutions" and the way they actually feel in daily life. If divorce by mutual consent becomes law, the press hails the event as "a great victory for freedom". But in practice I have yet to meet one divorced person celebrating a victory. At best it is an admission of failure; at worst it is a tragedy from which a person never recovers. Even when it is unavoidable, divorce is always painful.

Faced with these difficulties, some of our contemporaries are ingeniously manufacturing escape hatches. Several of these belong purely and simply to the realm of fantasy. The other day I heard on the radio a woman putting a lengthy case for communal living. Since it is a tragedy for children to lose one of their parents, she said, it would be much better for the third person in the triangle to come and live in the home. In that way you would have under the same roof five or six adults, some living together, others rejected, and eight or ten children. Human nature is infinitely flexible, this woman said, and if the social prejudice against such a solution were suppressed, it would be perfectly satisfactory. In fact, I happen to know personally children who have had to live in such a situation, and their lives bear the stamp of tragedy. As for jealousy, an objection which another participant raised, the speaker gave the large reply that it is not a fundamental component of human nature, but only the product of social prejudice.

Another suggestion is becoming more and more frequent — that since the advance of medicine has increased the length of human life, it is hopelessly idealistic to expect that two partners should remain faithful to each other for fifty years, and it is therefore inevitable that people should change partners from time to time. There is an even more radical idea: that since marriage so often fails, it should be abolished. In Sweden, for example, official forms no longer ask if you are married or not, but if you are co-habiting or not.

All these possibilities can be endlessly discussed. They can be opposed on the grounds of principle, tradition, morals, religion. Personally, I find in them a common weakness: they all reject one fundamental element, which is the possibility that everyone can change. And if I say to myself, "Utopia! He/she will never change!" there still remains the possibility of starting with myself. Why change partners if it is possible for both to become new people? Why separate if the selfishness which makes the situation intolerable can be broken?

I do not say this lightly. Our marriage, like most marriages, has been through two or three of those crises in which the horizon seems for ever closed. It was through change in human character — in the event, mine — that we emerged. Human beings are free. We can accept or refuse change. If we refuse, then we have to find other roads. But by denying the possibility of change, we slam the door in the face of hope and condemn ourselves to non-satisfying solutions.

These two stories of marriages remade are both — except for the names — true.

It was during the war. Jean was posted as an auxiliary nurse to the Far East, and there she met Robert, an attractive officer. Their romance developed rapidly and they were married. Neither of them knew much about the other's family background. In the tropics and under war conditions, that did not seem very important.

Robert was the only son of a widow, who had alternately spoiled and dominated him. Jean was too young to understand a man's complex reactions to such an upbringing. She herself had a high ideal of family life, and had decided as a girl that she would work hard at being a good wife and mother. After three months, she was honest enough to admit to herself that her marriage had been a mistake. But what should she do now? True to her upbringing and character, she decided to face the difficulties, to repress her feelings and to make the best of the situation. But underneath, resentment and self-pity began to gnaw.

Jean became pregnant and had to return to Europe. Her own family could not have her, so Robert arranged that she should go to his mother. When she arrived at her mother-in-law's house, tired after the long journey and feeling a little lost, she was welcomed with, "So you're the girl who's stolen my son?" It was said as a joke, but there was no mistaking the feelings behind the words.

The months that followed were among the worst of Jean's life. Beset with her own problems, she felt incapable of making the slightest effort to understand her mother-in-law, a nervy and volatile woman. So she wrote her off as an incorrigible tyrant, and began to react with sulky silences or angry words. Amazed at her own spitefulness, she said to herself, "She is undermining my real nature." Those difficult months became one more grievance against her husband.

At the end of the war, Robert came home. Jean continued to do what she thought was her duty. She brought up the children conscientiously and took care of her husband, but with a closed heart. He tried to care for her, but his difficult relationship with his mother had made him singularly distrustful of any sign of feminine domination. If Jean expressed one point of view, he inevitably adopted the opposite. One day he told her what a shock it had been to discover that the girl he had so idolised could have such a wicked tongue. She snapped back that it was living with him that had made her like that. The barrier of good behaviour gone, her frustration and rebellion burst out in violent scenes, until one day she threw herself on the ground and drummed the earth with her heels.

Jean kept going to church regularly, hoping that perhaps some sort of divine aid might rescue her. But there was no sign of it, and gradually she began to perceive the gulf between the person she had thought she was and the person she really was. Then she met a couple who made a deep impression on her. They were happy together, but they were quite open about the difficulties they had to surmount daily to get on with each other and to resolve the frictions which, in the long run, destroy a home. For months she was left with a sort of wistfulness. Then she met them again and glimpsed the key to the mystery: everyone has a destiny which you can discover step by step, but only if you stop blaming other people and face your own need of change.

This new perspective demanded from Jean a completely different attitude. The "divine aid" she had hoped for became more vital than ever, but it took on a much more down-to-earth character than she could have imagined. She had to decide to see herself as God saw her and to let him clean the places which needed it. She realised that by closing her heart to her husband she had robbed him of the affection, the understanding and the hope which were so necessary to him. But it was not enough to become aware of this; she had to learn, incident by incident, to live in a different way. Although her pride suffered, she had at last the impression of a gleam at the end of the tunnel. Instead of groping in the dark, she began to see the way again.

One day when her husband had been particularly rude and she felt the old angry reactions rising, instead of exploding at him she rushed to her bedroom, burst into tears, threw herself on her knees and said, "God, I don't have to tell you that I've got a difficult husband. But please tell me if I did anything to deserve such rough words." "Yes," came the very simple reply. "You were dead set on having things done your way."

She went to Robert and told him this, and added that she was sorry for being so stubborn. He smiled and underlined the point: "It's true, you really were dead set!"

An incident which a few months before would have turned into a scene, that day built a bridge — or at least a footbridge — between them.

The children were not slow to notice the difference. Their son, who had regularly been bottom of his class, moved to the top. His teacher wrote to the parents about his astonishment at their son's change of character and his progress. Even the relationship with Robert's mother took a new turn. Shortly before she died, Robert said to Jean, "You couldn't have taken better care of her if she had been your own mother."

Jean is now a widow. She says with a smile, "If I've learned one thing — and I paid dearly for the lesson — it is that the woman who's always right is always wrong! But she doesn't have to go on like that, and if she changes, everything can change."

Paul and Monica started their marriage on a much better footing. Despite the initial opposition of her family, they had a real harmony of background, culture and ideals. And they had in addition that deep feeling, which does not depend only on love, that their lives had been destined to come together.

He started off full of illusions about her, but his idealism was not of the dramatic sort, and he lost them little by little without traumas and without any lessening of affection for her.

She had fewer illusions about him, but one of them was rather large. She was convinced that, under her beneficial influence, he would without doubt improve considerably and lose some of the defects which she had noticed.

Months passed, then a year, then two, and the beneficial influence proved totally ineffective. After three years, Monica was forced to face the truth squarely — she would have to spend her whole life with her husband just as he was! The two or three character traits of his from which she particularly suffered appeared then a veritable Himalayan range. It was unbearable, something would have to give, but what? The marriage itself? To her it was indissoluble, and the question of divorce did not even arise. Her nerves? They were strong. And it only needed a glance at the seething floods of the neighbouring river to convince her that suicide was not her calling. There remained the prospect of an infinite succession of grey, disappointing days for — who knows? — ten, twenty, fifty years. She was too young to accept that.

Monica then remembered a phrase she had heard one day: "No problem can resist five minutes of absolute honesty." She went into a small chapel and there, telling herself that she had nothing to lose, she took a notebook and pen to play the game of honesty right to the end. She was in such inner turmoil that it was a good five minutes before the honesty began to do its work.

She has allowed me to quote here some of the thoughts that came to her: "Do you remember the day when you were ten and your parents quarrelled so? You swore then that if ever you married, your marriage would be a success. That's why you're so determined to reform your husband's character. But what sort of husband wants to be his wife's creation? Your husband has his own destiny, just like everyone else. It's up to you to help him to fulfil it.

"Your husband has a difficult character. You are not an easy woman either. It is impossible that your marriage should run smoothly. But when you are at the station with a case that is too heavy for you, what do you do? You get a porter. Don't forget that God is always there, ready to carry your burdens. You are going to find a new unity and give courage to many other couples.

"Tell your husband the truth. Tell your parents too."

Here, Monica says, she gave an indignant start. It was asking too much of her pride. Her parents would certainly say to her, "You see, we warned you!" But the ideas in the notebook formed such a coherent whole that it was difficult to leave out the last line. She went out of the chapel decided to complete the game. An open-hearted conversation with her husband, a letter to her parents — the hardest of her life — and in the space of twenty-four hours the Himalayas had disappeared. It was not the end of their difficulties, but it was like dawn breaking.

Happiness and success are not the only important elements in marriage. There is another which is vital, to give it both stability and joy. This is creation, in the broadest sense of the term.

This means the procreation of children, of course, with all the years of self-sacrifice that it presupposes until they become tomorrow's adults. But it also means the blossoming of the individual creative gifts of both the man and the woman, supported and encouraged by each other. And finally, it means the creative work that they can undertake together when they have a common commitment. It is often in this creative outlet to the world that marriage finds its deepest meaning and fulfilment. In his novel *Manalive*, G.K. Chesterton makes this recommendation to girls: "Stick to the man who looks out of the window and tries to understand the world. Keep clear of the man who looks in at the window and tries to understand you."[5] This remark is full of profound wisdom. Love suffocates in a jar.

To help the other person to fulfil their individual destiny is one of the greatest tokens of love that you can give. And it can demand considerable selflessness.

Disraeli once had to make an important speech in the House of Commons. His wife came to support him, as she often did. They climbed into the carriage that was to take them to Parliament, and the coachman slammed the door on her fingers. She nearly fainted; her husband, absorbed in preparing for his speech, noticed nothing. Mrs Disraeli settled in the corner of the carriage, nursed her hand and said not a word about it, as she did not want her husband to worry about her when he had affairs of state on his mind.

Most of us will probably not have to display such heroism, but the point is clear for every husband and every wife in the world. Wives know only too well that it can even require sacrifice to make sure that their husbands have a clean shirt at the required moment!

But there are some sacrifices that husband and wife must make together. I know several couples who have taken on the specialised education of delinquent or predelinquent children. Their lives are hardly their own; they belong to the children, who look to them for what they have desperately lacked in their own families. Their own children, whose immediate interests sometimes seem to be overlooked, do not suffer in the long run because, thanks to their parents' common commitment, they have the security of living in deeply united homes.

"For better for worse, till death us do part." This insistence on personal faithfulness is a deep spring that can transform society. No society can function without the incorruptible person, faithful to his given word, who puts other people's interests before his own. In all corners of the earth, in East and West, in industrialised and in developing countries, in Communist and in capitalist societies, there is a search for such people. Perhaps it is from the intimate relationship of love and faithfulness, freely chosen, that this type of person arises. If husband and wife are faithful to each other, if those who know them learn this faithfulness, then we can have politicians faithful to their electors, industrialists faithful to their workers, trade unionists faithful to the brotherhood of man.

An intimate and privileged relationship can be a source of general good. It is worth thinking about. Writing off faithfulness in marriage means the risk of writing off the trust without which collective life does not succeed. Faithfulness in love can lay the foundations for the fulfilment of our deepest hopes for the future of our children and our nations.

Notes
[1] William Shakespeare: *Romeo and Juliet*, Act II, Scene II.
[2] Matthew 19, 6 (J.B. Phillips' translation).
[3] Larry Christenson: *The Christian Family*, Bethany Fellowship, 1971, p. 29.
[4] Michel Quoist: *The Christian Response*, Gill and Macmillan, 1965, p. 121.
[5] G.K. Chesterton: *Manalive*, Darwen Finlayson, 1962, p. 188.

10

A Motherhood Explosion

The French women's magazine *Marie-Claire*[1] carried an article on "Woman, the unknown". The author's argument went like this: for the first time in human history, thanks to the development of contraceptive techniques, woman now has the freedom to choose whether she wants to be a mother; therefore, after thousands of years during which the feminine condition has been irrevocably bound up with motherhood, we are now going to be able to discover what a woman really is.

This argument is, in my opinion, somewhat acrobatic. Dragging a boat on to dry land is not necessarily the best way to discover its true characteristics. And if it is limiting to consider woman only in relation to biological motherhood, perhaps interesting discoveries could be made by studying motherhood in all its dimensions — biological, human and spiritual, global.

There exists, obviously, a purely animal maternal instinct which we share with mammals, birds and even reptiles, and which exceeds in intensity the instinct for self-preservation, fundamental as that is. Animals risk their lives to defend their young; and many mothers in occupied France pretended that they were not hungry so that their children could eat a little more. This instinct is so powerful because it is essential to the survival of the species. If the animal mother and her young did not find pleasure in mutual physical contact, the young would get lost and be eaten by the first predator to come across it. And human mothers know perfectly well that if we did not feel that our baby was king of the world, we should not have the necessary patience to wash his nappies, put up with his nonsense and devote fifteen or twenty years of our lives to bringing him up.

In animals, the maternal instinct is contained within precise limits and usually disappears after weaning. The upbringing of human young lasts much longer, and also poses the problem not simply of bringing up an adult capable of surviving alone, but of producing a social being. In a primitive tribe, to be able to integrate in the group a child needs to learn the tribal customs, rites and taboos. In our so-called civilised society, the number of things the child has to learn before he can take his final place is quite stupefying when you stop to think about it.

Things are further complicated by the fact that, these days, there is no general consensus on what standards are basic to our civilisation. A young African woman once said to me, "It must be so difficult for you to bring up children! With us, everyone is agreed what they should learn, and all the children learn from all the adults. Any man or woman in the village can correct a child, and you know they will tell him exactly the same as his own parents would tell him. And the children give equal respect to all their elders. But in your country everyone has their own ideas, and nobody can guess what anyone else wants their child to learn. So you are left on your own to bring up your own children. Each family has its own favourite coffee and its own favourite system of bringing-up!"

There is also a deeper question. How will the child of today — the adult of tomorrow — use the free choice that being human confers on him? Will he be a server or an exploiter? A Socialist women's leader was once addressing an audience of students. She announced that she was going to speak on exploitation, which subject was greeted with much joy by the students, who held strong political views. "The first sort of exploitation I should like to talk about," she said, "is the exploitation of parents by students." There was general consternation, but her audience took in every word.

In a world in which we are more and more interdependent, it is useless to hope that any individual can jog along in his own sweet way without affecting anyone else. Either we put ourselves at the service of the fullest blossoming of the other person, the other race, the other class, the other country, or else we put them at the service of our comfort, our profit, our power-seeking. The child who does not learn to serve learns to exploit.

As parents we feel our responsibility for this choice; but how to fulfil that responsibility? Instinct is no sure guide; the patterns which our parents have bequeathed to us seem out-of-date, overtaken by the evolution of the modern world. The books and theories of experts contradict each other endlessly. Is there a guide anywhere?

There are two truths which I believe can help. The first is that we actually pass on to our children only those values in which we deeply believe. Our words and good intentions weigh very little against the reality of our lives as seen by the watching child. In fact, we are probably the best educators not when we are trying to educate, but when we react simply and instinctively in a crisis. The child watches, draws his own conclusions and never forgets.

I know a young Australian who was brought up in a farming family with little money. At the end of one particularly difficult year, on Christmas Day, there was almost nothing to eat in the house. He was eight. His mother, as she served the meagre dinner she had cooked, said to him, "You see, son, this year we have obviously not given enough." The lesson in generosity, and in confidence in life, was impressed for ever on the boy.

The second truth is that we can cultivate a seed so that it produces a tree and the tree bears fruit, but the seed is not made by us. The child is born with an immense potential, made up of gifts and lack of gifts, strong points and weak points, possibilities for good and for evil. He is also born with an inner instrument which enables him to distinguish between good and evil. This is conscience, but it is more than conscience: it is the inner compass, so sensitive and so accurate.

It is the accepted thing today to deny the existence of this innate conscience. It is said, and constantly repeated in every possible way, that morality is a cultural superstructure, invented out of nothing and imposed on the individual from outside. Of course there are hypocrites who try to impose a moral code which they fail to practise. But that is a long way from saying that they originated it.

However widely the customs of one country differ from those of its neighbours — Britain and France are a prime example — the similarities in basic values are even more striking; and these similarities span centuries as well as national borders. Passages from the literature of antiquity speak to us with remarkable freshness and bear out the fact that from one millenium to another, from one continent to another, human nature is astonishingly alike. Respect for promises and for other people's lives and property, purity, courage, selfless love, faithfulness in love and in friendship, sacrifice — these are values too universal to have emerged haphazardly.

They correspond to something deeper: that grain of conscience which the child brings with him when he is born. Modern education insists on the development of individual gifts — music, mathematics, drawing, mechanics, gardening. But the most precious of all gifts, the one which allows us to distinguish between good and evil and to choose good, is the one that most needs to be nourished, encouraged and cultivated. That is the gift that makes us truly free and truly equal.

The existence of this compass — of this inner voice — is a fact tested by countless people. The test consists in being silent and allowing the inner voice to speak, instead of our own specious arguments which allow us to do what we want. Then the voice speaks, simply, clearly, to the child and to the adult.

One small boy, like many other small boys and most cats, hated soap. For ten minutes he stood stamping in front of the basin, refusing to wash. His mother, annoyed, left the room. Then she heard a voice calling, "Mummy, who is it saying to me, 'Wash your face, wash your face!'?" The little boy recognised the inner voice and washed his face without any more fuss. He was two and a half.

Of course, self-will does not always give up so easily. A small French girl, whose mother had suggested being quiet to listen to the inner voice, looked up from under her lashes and said, "It talks to me in English and I don't understand." It turned out, of course, that the voice had spoken clearly and in excellent French!

One mother I know, encouraged by experiences like this, decided that she would always be as exacting with her children as their own consciences, realising that every compromise which she allowed diminished the force of this inner guide in her children. It was a difficult decision. There is always the moment when you are tired or upset, or there is a visitor, and the child plays up. But one day he will be grateful that the just authority of his parents echoed his own inner compulsion.

A conscious decision to develop this faculty of free choice in our children is a guarantee against one of the strongest temptations of motherhood — to consider that our children "belong" to us and to try to control their development according to our own wishes, our own rights, perhaps even our own frustrations. A friend of mine who is a headmaster tells me that parents even bring him small boys of seven and announce that this one is going to university or that one will take up a career in the Navy.

Freedom needs a framework in which to develop. In a moving book, Denise Herbaudière tells the epic of her education of her handicapped daughter. In the final chapter she writes something which applies equally to a normal child: "Paradoxically, learning freedom, autonomy and initiative comes from an outside authority. You can only give autonomy to a reasonable being. Autonomy develops through self-control, and I make up for lapses in this through an emergency outside control, so that autonomy does not degenerate into chaos. Some professionals find it difficult to understand that everything that weakens self control, such as unbridled permissiveness, militates against the growth of autonomy. . . Of course I have to fix limits which take into account the family 'group law' and the needs of other people, but freedom which is exercised even within a restricted framework is still freedom, and I can extend its limits as my daughter's power over herself develops."[2]

Children understand, accept and even like these limits. One mother I know, exasperated by her six-year-old son who had been dawdling in his bath for a quarter of an hour, lost patience and gave him a resounding smack on the behind. When he went to bed, the red mark of her hand with its five fingers was still visible, and she was not very proud of herself. Nevertheless, objectively speaking, the child had overstepped the bounds. She said to him, "I don't know if it's a good thing or a bad thing, but there is a limit to the patience of mothers. You went beyond that limit and that's why you got a smack." The boy thought about it, and then remarked philosophically, "I rather think it's a good thing."

Children, and especially adolescents, may fiercely oppose the limits set for them. But make no mistake. Very often they want not so much to have the rules set aside as to see if the adult holds firm and really believes in the principle behind the rule. A Canadian friend of mine has brought up four sons, now grown men. One of the rules of family life was that at the age of fifteen the boy must be home by midnight. Each of the boys in turn rebelled against this rule, but had to obey it. One day, the son who was fifteen at the time was talking about one of his friends. "Poor Richard!" he said. "His parents don't really love him, they let him stay out till all hours!"

There is also a totally different dimension of motherhood which is too rarely considered. All of us know women, married or single, who are mothers to a whole district, to a town, or to a nation. And I have met astonishing women who, as teachers, manage to be mothers to hundreds of children and even to their parents.

One of my closest friends is Irène Laure, formerly head of the three million Socialist women of France. Even as a child she had a passion for looking after people. She used to take clothes from her father — a factory owner who in her opinion had more than enough clothes — and give them to his workers if they were ill or in want. At 14, she spent all her pocket-money and her spare time in looking after young unmarried mothers. She and her husband, with five children of their own, adopted nine others, including a German boy. When war broke out, she became a leader of the Resistance, and one of her own sons was tortured by the Gestapo. After the war, when she found herself face to face with Germans again, she rebelled and closed her heart to them. But she realised that the dreams of Socialism — the brotherhood of man in a world at peace — would not be born that way. And for the sake of her grandchildren and the world's grandchildren, she apologised to the Germans for her hatred, not once but hundreds of times, all over postwar Germany. The French Foreign Minister said that she had done more than any other person to lay the foundations for the new trust between France and Germany. And since then her heart has taken in the whole world.

As her interpreter, I have seen her treat recalcitrant American Senators and the poorest American Indians as her own children. In a few hours — sometimes in a few minutes — she unearths the problems, fears and hopes of the people she meets. She boils with impatience at Christians whose faith begins and ends with words. She believes that once you have touched a problem, you work at its solution; and if you have a faith, you should be ten times more effective than those who have not. From Calcutta's homeless to Congolese rebels, from Vietnam to Brazil, all are her own children. Where she has been — and she stays not one or two days, but five or six months — social transformations begin.

And the rest of us, unexceptional women as most of us are, have our part to play in this "global motherhood". Michel Quoist writes: "The modern world was built without woman. It suffers from the lack of a mother. It is inhuman as a result. . . What woman is for man in the building of a home, she must also be for society in the building of the world. The life of woman is one of openness; openness to man, to her child, to her home and family. She must be in the world, for it is she whose thoughts are absorbed with the life of man, it is she who listens to his deepest aspirations, those beyond mere physical need."[3]

It is only in that perspective that being a mother takes on its full meaning.

Notes
[1] August 1975.
[2] Denise Herbaudière: *Cati ou l'enfance muette*, Mercure de France, 1972, p. 285.
[3] Michel Quoist, op. cit., pp. 22, 23.

11

Home

In 1975, Simone de Beauvoir, the foremost French "women's liberationist", was interviewed for the first time on television. She was asked, "Having successfully campaigned for contraception and abortion, what will your next campaign be about?" She answered without the slightest hesitation, "Housework. We are going to organise strikes against housework." And this subject is, in fact, one of the chief ideological issues of our age.

The respective role of the sexes in household responsibilities has become a fashionable subject for discussion. A few years ago, I saw in Paris a play called *The Brat*. The curtain rose on a typical family breakfast at home. The first shock came when the young mother, on the dot of 7.30, left for work. She was a crane driver. Father and uncle stayed behind to mind the baby and do the housework. This they had arranged to suit themselves beautifully. They played cards and relaxed until four in the afternoon; then with typical masculine efficiency they dealt with dishes, dirt and diapers, and mother returned from her crane at 5.30 to find everything spick and span. This perfect domestic arrangement was disturbed when young uncle brought home a bride who did not fancy crane driving, and insisted on vacuum cleaning at nine in the morning.

This play was a sign of the times. I thought it wildly exaggerated then. But not long ago a young man told me quite seriously that he wanted to take a break of two or three years in his career to do what he liked most — housekeeping and cooking. And to be quite sure we are not "sexist", we talk seriously of changing the primary school books and replacing the little girl in the classic apron, making pastry at her mother's side, by a little girl in dungarees armed with a plane in a carpenter's shop.

What is completely lost in this controversy is the real meaning of housework and of home-making. A woman I know well lived in a not very comfortable house in a poor area. Almost every afternoon her son brought his friends home to play after school. One day, somewhat irritated by all the muddy feet and noisy comings and goings on the staircase, she asked her son, "Why do you always bring your friends here? Why don't you ever go to one of their homes?" Her son, after a moment's thought, replied, "Well, you see, first, you give them each a biscuit. And then, you always want me."

To me this reply sums up perfectly the deep sense of home — the gesture and the welcome. The gesture, because in a home it is neither theories nor words that speak loudest — in fact, they are quickly seen through. What counts is the true gesture — the biscuit — that has cost something in effort, imagination, service. And then the welcome. "You always want me." The open door, not only for the family, but for the neighbourhood and for the whole world. The welcome, which is costly because your plans and your comfort are constantly disturbed, but which means that the person nearest you or the stranger can come in at any time, lay down his burden and find the strength and the vision to continue on his way.

If that is what really counts in the creation of a home — the gesture which expresses an unselfish and loving intention, and the welcome without limits or barriers — then this is an art, and a lifetime is not long enough to learn and practise it.

One of my single friends has had a highly successful career as a musician and teacher in the South of France. She lived in a university town where there were 7,000 foreign students. In her flat she had a sitting-room, a piano and twenty-five chairs and stools, and she decided to put these assets to use. In the next few years 3,500 foreign students were not only received for the first time in a French home, but they found someone who listened to them and could sometimes help them to lose their loneliness and their fears for their countries.

The disturbances of May 1968, when all over France

students demonstrated violently on behalf of the workers, profoundly affected the school where she was teaching. One evening she invited to her home one of the leaders of the student movement and a retired trade-unionist from Paris who, she hoped, would help the young man to grasp some of the realities of the workers' struggle. The conversation was going well, with arguments flying to and fro like ping-pong balls in a championship. Suddenly there was a ring at the door — an unexpected visit from the Vicar-General of the diocese. He was at once included and, in the warmth of that living home, these men — from different backgrounds and generations — were able to listen to each other and learn from each other. In the course of the evening, the student admired a wooden cross from Florence, which my friend herself loved dearly. As they were leaving, she decided to give it to him. He put it carefully in a chocolate wrapper. When he went away, he took with him, as well as his treasure, a new idea of what life could hold. As for the Vicar-General, he had met people and views such as rarely came into his orbit.

Another friend of mine lives near the port of London. One year a national strike of seamen started at the same time as she started her spring cleaning. The loose covers of the sitting-room furniture had just gone to the cleaners, when her husband came home and told her that he had invited one of the strike committee for supper that evening, with some friends who might be able to help with the deadlock in the ports. She was very concerned about the strike, and its impact on the seamen's families as well as on the country, but she could not help feeling her husband might have chosen a more convenient time to get involved.

However, she had decided to say "yes" instead of "no" when apparently impossible things were asked of her. So the manager of the cleaners was enlisted, and a mechanic found to repair one of their machines which had just broken down. The sitting-room was reconstituted. Jean, aged twelve, baked biscuits. And the evening's discussions, which gave the seamen's leader fresh perspective and courage, provided the impetus for new negotiations which three weeks later brought a solution. My friend said to me afterwards, "Housework isn't slavery when you have an aim in life. In fact, it helps you to reach your aim. And for an evening like that, all of us in the family help. So the work seems worth it."

Life in such a home cannot be boring. In any case, to be a good housewife and mother requires expertise in a daunting number of skilled professions — child welfare, education, dietetics, cooking, pastry-making, laundering, dyeing, ironing, carpentry, joinery, electricity, plumbing, physics and chemistry, economics and accountancy, painting, decorating, medicine — for a start. And what is more, you have to be able to leap from one profession to another at a moment's notice without losing your head.

What really matters is the intention behind the housework. A well-polished tile floor can convey any number of different meanings: "I have done my duty", "I am afraid of what my mother-in-law would think if she turned up unexpectedly", "I am not like my neighbour who neglects her housework", "Life is good and deserves a well-polished floor". Oddly, although it is the same floor, you can sense very quickly which of these messages it is conveying. You either feel at home in a house full of satisfaction and cheerfulness, or you feel vaguely guilty at putting your feet on a masterpiece.

In one of his books, Laurens van der Post writes: "There is a profound interdependence of world without and world within, and experience in either one of them is valid also in the other. Whenever one succeeds in breaking the code wherein their meaning is transmitted from one dimension to the other, this validity is so marked that one wonders whether they are really two different dimensions and not just two aspects of one and the same whole. The visible world being merely the spirit seen from without; the spirit, just the world without seen from within."[1]

He is writing about the people, the animals and the plants of his beloved Africa, but we can equally apply what he says to our homes. It is up to us to "break the code" which links the world without to the world within.

The gift of limitless welcome is rarely natural to a housewife. It is more often the result of discipline and training. These are sometimes imposed from outside by the cultural background, as in Arab and African countries, sometimes chosen from within. For me, a Western woman in a town, the temptation to self-sufficiency is extraordinarily strong. If you give in to it, the unexpected visitor becomes the upsetter of plans, and you get into the vicious circle of individualism and isolation.

I have had to learn how to let my heart speak more loudly than my sense of organisation. One day when I was in the middle of some housework with a scarf tied on anyhow, there was a ring at the door, and there stood a young couple whom we had got to know a year previously and who were about to leave the city. Instead of welcoming them and apologising for the disorder in the flat, I froze, and then I said, "You didn't tell me you were coming this morning, did you?" Nothing I could do succeeded in dispelling the embarrassment caused by my first reaction. In the first second the person standing on the threshold knows whether he is welcome or not. There is no time to prepare. The welcome must be right there, available, instantaneous, as much a part of you as your own skin. The shame I still feel at the memory of that incident has saved me from many pitfalls since.

I learned another lesson in hospitality in a community home in Paris. We had staying there some Koreans who had suffered cruelly under the occupation of the Japanese and had newly decided to forgive them. Their story was so moving that it deeply touched all the Japanese who heard it, and we wanted some of those living in Paris to meet the Koreans.

It was a warm summer day, and we planned a dinner in the garden for eight o'clock. At half past seven everything was ready. The small tables outside and the large buffet in the dining-room were splendidly laid out. At that moment the telephone rang — five more people coming to dinner. A table had to be added, so I set about the task with as much good grace as I could muster. At five to eight everything was once again perfectly arranged. The telephone rang once more. A table for six must be added. Again the magnificent arrangement of china and silver would have to be disturbed. This time I had no good grace left, and I stood paralysed with frustration in the middle of the dining-room. I had reached the limits of my hospitality.

Someone else came to the rescue, a table was added, and the guests arrived to a scene of peace and order. The lanterns were lit in the garden, and after coffee we gathered in the library to talk. It was an unforgettable evening, and I had to admit to myself that the last-minute guests were the ones who got the most out of it.

This raises the subject of community living as opposed to the restricted family unit. I have myself lived in a community, first as a single woman, then as a married one and finally as a mother. For me, this experience of community life was totally positive, but only because certain conditions were fulfilled. First, we had a common ideal and common aims larger than the community itself. In addition, we had accepted in advance that the quality and quantity of service which community living would demand of us would be greater than in a restricted family.

So many communal experiments have failed because of the basic illusion that "there will be more shoulders to carry my burden", whether the burden is the housework or existence itself. In practice the opposite happens. We had to learn to strengthen our own shoulders to carry the burdens of others, otherwise there was the inevitable exploitation of some by others — of the unmarried by the married, for instance, or vice versa — and the door was wide open for criticism, comparison and bitterness. If human relations are the essence of family life, those relations will be more complex in a community than in a traditional family. But because of this, successful community life is a source of infinite wealth.

Homes may be small or large, but they give the people who live in them a definite place in society — something which everyone needs. To have a place implies restrictions, but it also confers a dignity without which we meander lost through the world. Before we women totally reject our privileged place in the home, with its drudgery and its joy, we need to think twice about what we are going to be and do instead, and to make sure not only that we will gain by the change, but that the world will gain.

Note
[1] Laurens van der Post: *A Far-Off Place*, Hogarth Press, 1974, p. 153.

12

Work?

This is going to be a chapter of question-marks, and for one simple reason. Women's work has been the subject of so many studies, so many commissions, so many statistics and so many controversies that there is little point in adding my shovelful to the mountain. But after meeting members of commissions, thumbing through statistics and listening to discussions, I have come to the conclusion that some of the fundamental questions have never been asked. And this is what I would like to try and do.

There is one important preliminary point. For the vast majority of women, there are no questions about work. It simply has to be done. The Asian woman stooping over a ricefield; the African woman cultivating her plot of cassava in the bush; the girl catching a bus in the morning to go to a cotton-mill in Bolton; the doctor spending long hours using the training which took her long years; the single woman with family responsibilities; the married woman who lives in conditions which make it impossible to manage on one person's pay — none of these women has the leisure or the opportunity for the luxury of questions. For them, work is part of life, like eating and drinking; and in this they are no different from men. Ménie Grégoire in her book[1] remarks that the feminine condition is neither a curse from which women must try to free themselves at any price, nor a vocation to the level of which they must raise themselves by dint of tremendous efforts, but quite simply a state, their state. This commonsense remark can be applied to work as well.

Complications do arise, of course, since women, as well as working, have to give birth to children and bring them up. In some cases the conflict is not very acute. I have been able to see and understand a little of life in an African village, as my African friend had already described it to me. There the mother gets on with her work while she carries her baby on her back. Later, he plays on the ground beside her. As well, any adult seeing a child in mischief or in danger feels at liberty to intervene, so the child is protected from all sides. Even in a town in Africa, the links of the extended tribal family are still close, and the mother can always find an adult or a young girl to help her. In Asia too, children belong to the whole community in a sense that is unknown to our individualistic Western society. The questions so keenly asked are in fact peculiar to the Western urban world, and are as well emotively tinged by the campaign for women's liberation. This is where my forest of question-marks begins to sprout.

First, is professional work as liberating for a woman as it is said to be? At the time of the first stammerings of feminism, G.K. Chesterton remarked on the thousands of women who, having protested against being dictated to, rushed off to take jobs as shorthand-typists. Seriously, I do not see why, for example, a mother looking after young children at home is a slave while a nursery-school teacher, doing exactly the same work with the same children, is "liberated". I see only two real differences: the teacher leaves her home and meets colleagues, and she gets her money from the body running the school instead of from her husband. Isn't it worth questioning the axiom that it is the pay that makes work liberating? Equal pay for equal work is just and necessary. But after justice has been established, we might ask whether work is devalued by lack of money or by lack of love.

Some kinds of work are easier to love than others, but that is too easy an excuse. Viktor Frankl writes: "Man should not ask what he may expect from life, but should rather understand that life expects something from him... Life is putting its problems to him, and it is up to him to respond to these questions by being responsible."[2] We know that Frankl does not speak lightly. He had to apply this philosophy to hard labour in a concentration camp. Popular wisdom puts it another way: "Happiness is not doing what you like but liking what you do."

I do not particularly envy the work of a salesgirl in a department store. But when I heard a girl who was paid both salary and commission say to her colleague, "Last month I worked because I wanted to buy myself a coat; this month I'm resting", I wondered whether she was not devaluing her own work. She was quite happily earning her salary by sitting on a stool and paying not the least attention to the customers at her counter. Doesn't work get its value as much from what we put into it as from what we get out of it?

I know a woman who had quite a senior administrative post. As a result of changes within the firm, she was demoted to a subordinate position where she was responsible for some correspondence which she did not find particularly interesting. She fell into "I couldn't care less", which was soon followed by bitterness. One day, disgusted with herself, she decided to give her best, even to the jobs which seemed to her least rewarding. Not only did she start enjoying her work again but, as a bonus, she was promoted.

It is still rare to find a woman who has the choice of the whole gamut of solutions: to stay at home, to work part-time, to work full-time or to do all of these in turn. But even when this becomes normal — and I hope it will be sooner rather than later — this outward freedom may not be enough to ensure true freedom. Don't we still have to reckon with the fundamental question of motives?

I once took part in a survey on "Woman, free to choose". Two young Parisians, each the mother of two children, gave interestingly varied views. One of them said, "You don't exactly have a knife at your throat when you decide to go out and work rather than stay at home. But there is the social pressure — the magazines, always harping on status, beautiful clothes, and all that. A mother, who is actually building lives, gets written off, while a surgeon, for instance, gets all the praise. It's not fair. But I do go out to work. I've decided I want a house of our own, space for the children and holidays at the seaside. I feel I'm contradicting myself inside — it's terrible!"

The other said, "If I have the chance to be or do something outside my home, I don't look at it as a right but as a way I can help someone else. So looking after other people, or looking after my husband and children, comes to the same thing. Life is a whole and is deeply satisfying. No woman today can be concerned with her home without becoming concerned with the society and the world where her home belongs. In one way or another she has to take responsibility, either by opening her own home to the world, or by answering a need outside her home.

"I don't think children suffer from being in a crèche, or being looked after by a helper or a grandmother, at some point in their lives, if their mother is away for a good reason. But it hurts me to think of the women who are forced to work and to put their children out to care because they really don't have enough to live on, and of the others who do it because their longing for possessions is a bottomless well, and because they always manage to compare themselves wtih the neighbour who has more and never with the one who has less."[3]

"Life is a whole and is deeply satisfying" — that is a phrase I like. It comes from one of those balanced women who know how to make real homes of the places where they work, and how to achieve a real work in their homes.

There is a certain interaction between our private motives and those which drive society in general. The press and the other media do amplify all sorts of innate tendencies, and rouse in us fears, desires and ambitions that we would never have thought of ourselves. On the other hand, public opinion is made up of the sum of our personal desires and individual choices.

One television discussion brought this home clearly to me. In front of an audience specially selected to form a hostile majority — the programme was called "Controversy"[4] — a pediatrician pleaded the cause of the mother at home. There was a certain weakness in her position, because she was considering mother and children as an entity in themselves, outside the context of material needs or the realities of the contemporary world. Even so, I was dumbfounded when a writer — a man — calmly explained to her that since modern society regards the creation of material objects and wellbeing as more important than the creation of people, women want to take part in this trend by manufacturing things instead of staying at home and looking after their children. If that is true, I thought, don't the values of contemporary society need to be turned upside down?

I was also troubled by the thought that women are racing to catch up with an industrial revolution already out-dated, and I could not help saying to myself, "Will we always be one revolution too late?" In the highly technical age we have now entered, the difficulties rarely come from things — there seems to be nothing we cannot discover or invent — but rather from human failings which stop the machine from working. The next revolution which will prove necessary, which is already proving necessary, will happen in human hearts and motives. That is the domain where our greatest gifts lie. Isn't it the moment to realise this and not to let ourselves, this time, be outrun?

In a family, a child needs a father and a mother. He would not know what to do with two fathers. It is the same in the world of work. Society is a joint creation of man and woman, and each must make a particular contribution. This does not mean that women should simply return to their traditional role. It does mean a way of being, in every situation in which women find themselves. The wife of a European politician puts it like this:

"Now, when it would be easy for her to become another man, woman must make absolutely clear the emotional and spiritual characteristics which distinguish her. Instead of duplicating man's race for profit, knowledge, power, woman should be a counterweight, so that the element of humanity tips the scales — so that everything which cannot be seen, cannot be measured, is not profitable and serves no useful purpose, but for lack of which humanity threatens to die, once again comes first."[5]

Notes
[1] Ménie Grégoire: *Le métier de femme*, Plon, Paris, 1965.

[2] Viktor E. Frankl: *The Doctor and the Soul: From Psychotherapy to Logotherapy,* tr. Richard and Clare Winston, Souvenir Press, 1969, p. xv.
[3] *Tribune de Caux*, Geneva, February 1974.
[4] BBC 2, 27 October 1975.
[5] Mme Hélène Guisan, Switzerland.

13

One Woman's Europe

A sister-in-law of mine found herself sitting at a lunch next to Jean Rey, at that time President of the Commission of the European Community. She showed him a document she had drawn up with other women in Britain, a "Housewives' Declaration" in which they pledged themselves to adopt a responsible attitude towards the vast economic problems of the country. Mr Rey read some of its points:
"We will care about the standard of living and true happiness of families across the world. Have we the right to get richer every year when so many are hungry?
"We will shop from need and not from greed or from hoarding and will rethink how much is enough for us.
"We will refuse to let the hurts and bitterness of entrenched attitudes of the past shape our future."
"You know what they say in Brussels?" he remarked with a smile. "That in Britain it's not the government that makes the decisions but the housewives."
It starts you dreaming. Could the mothers, the housewives, the women really transform the attitudes of Europe? What would it mean, what would it cost us?
When I try to define Europe in my own mind, I think not so much of our geography as of our heritage. We have a very long family history, going back to the blossoming of the Mediterranean civilisations, taking in the empires which have come and gone, the barbarians, the explorers, the saints and scientists.
The golden threads of our ideals and blood-red threads of our rivalries, which form the fabric of Europe, form as well, I sometimes feel, the fabric of my own life. Both my grandfathers came from Alsace, that part of the continent

which has been a battle-field ever since the days of Charlemagne's grandsons. In that green and beautiful countryside, which France and Germany have fought over during the centuries like divorced parents fighting over their child, my father's family have been farmers and brewers from generation to generation, and the family house still stands on the church square in La Petite Pierre. I have inherited the characteristic Teutonic stubbornness of Alsace, known there as "square-headedness". I grew up, with all that youthful patriotism which marks you for life, as a Frenchwoman. My classical studies have given me that Latin mind which has its home around the Mediterranean. Now, my husband, my son and my home are English, and I am becoming steeped in a culture which is both Celtic and Anglo-Saxon, and which is the cradle of those nearest to me in life.

Through three wars, my family has been torn apart between France and Germany. During the last war, five of my grandmother's family died in the gas chambers of Dachau. Many of my friends were killed, some in the Resistance, some trying to escape into Spain, some while they were being deported to Germany, some on the battlefields of Normandy.

The Liberation came when I was nineteen, just as I was about to start my last year of classics at the Sorbonne and to try my hand at teaching. The upheavals our country had been through had completely changed my view of the future. I tried to see the sense in all these tragedies. What use were they? We had dreamed that France would be a happy country when the Germans left, but she was already tearing herself to pieces in the purges. Was this what all the suffering had led to? I was ready for a cause, or rather — for there are so many petty causes — an ideology.

One day in November 1944 our door-bell rang, and there stood an English army captain who had been given our address by friends. Our preoccupations at that time were rather basic, and I looked longingly at his khaki haversack, hoping that it held some of those army rations which to us meant culinary paradise. My parents took him into the sitting-room, and he opened it up. Disappointment! Not a single bite of food — nothing but books, pamphlets, newspapers. But I have never been able to resist a printed page. And besides, after four years of isolation and lying propaganda, we were famished for anything from "outside". I hardly noticed that all this literature was about Moral Re-Armament — it was enough that it came from Britain and America.

At the end of three days I had read every word. And I had discovered practical patriotism. Several times I had found the phrase, "As I am, so is my nation." France would be what the French made of her; but the French would be no different from what I was prepared to become. If I wanted France to be honest, united, clean, there had to be a revolution in my own quality of life and my own motives. It was so simple. There was even a small newspaper written by children of ten to twelve. Their stories were about the decisions they had taken to help their country. One had stopped pinching jam from his mother's cupboard; another had given up lounging in bed after the alarm had gone off. Childish? Of course — it was a children's paper. But it bore the mark of real solutions, simple and difficult at the same time.

The following year I found myself in England, seeing Moral Re-Armament in action there. A year later, degree in pocket, I arrived at Caux, the international centre of Moral Re-Armament which the Swiss had just opened. And there my life found its direction. The part played by Caux in the reconciliation of Europe, the reconstruction of the post-war world and the great crises of decolonisation belongs to history and has no place here. For myself, I learned my lesson: it matters little being first or last, playing a big part or a minute part, provided you are in a battle large enough to meet the world's needs.

But the lesson was not an easy one. Like most of my generation in France, by 1945 I had acquired a firm hatred not only of Hitlerite Germany but simply of Germany. These feelings seemed so amply justified that I did not take the trouble to examine them or their far-reaching consequences.

At Caux, I had to share a room with two German women. One had never followed Hitler, the other had been a Nazi youth leader. We went through every possible phase from superficial politeness through armed neutrality to explosions of deep anger, in discussions which lasted till the small hours.

Then came the moment of truth. In the autumn of 1948 I was asked by some Germans to come to their country, with others of various nationalities who were also at Caux. I was determined never to set foot in Germany, and I sent my suitcase off to Paris. It was three months before I saw it again, three months which were decisive not only for me personally, but for many Germans who found a new road during that time. I shall never forget the welcome we were given, the beds provided for us in homes where there were not even enough beds for the family, the loaves of grey bread so generously shared. And yet all this healed nothing in my heart, full of fear, of inborn mistrust and of the desire to destroy today those who had destroyed us yesterday.

One day I was asked to speak at a meeting in Ulm Cathedral. We were travelling to Ulm along a new motorway, and I could not help thinking of my friends who had built it under forced labour. To crown it all, we passed a signpost which said "Dachau". I was being forced to a choice: either I was going to remain imprisoned in my bitterness about the past, or I was going to let it go so that the future might be different.

But though I could see the choice clearly enough, I was absolutely incapable of controlling the tumult of my feelings. The inner compass, with its built-in resistance to magnetic storms, came to my rescue. Into my mind came very clearly the words I should say in the cathedral — words of forgiveness, which might reach the hearts and consciences of the Germans. The only trouble was that I simply did not want to say those words. We were driving through the hills and forests of Bavaria on a brilliant October day. I had just an hour to decide, then half an hour. Then I realised that, even if I was unable to master my feelings, I still had the freedom to speak or not to speak these words. It was a choice of my will. I decided finally to opt for the future.

As the days went by, I was amazed to discover that I saw Germany through different eyes. As well as what she had been, I saw what she could become, and I found myself ready to fight to the limit of my strength for this to come true. The story of what happened in Germany during that journey is beyond the scope of this book; it is written elsewhere.[1] But it taught me that public reconciliations like the one between France and Germany, which is now part of contemporary history, grow from private revolutions in the hearts of ordinary women.

With Britain the problem is more subtle. It is not a question of enmity, but of rivalry. For centuries, in Canada, in India, on the high seas and in distant deserts, Britain and France have struggled for leadership. Even the comradeship of two world wars has not resolved the inherited rivalries. Dunkirk means one thing in Britain, quite another in France. The Frenchman insists on asserting his superiority; the Englishman is so certain of his that he does not even bother to assert it, which only exasperates us the more. This rivalry was so real to me that just six months before my engagement I was banging on the table and saying, "Never, never, never will I marry an Englishman!"

Shortly after our engagement, we were lunching with a diplomat who had just spent three years with the Organisation for Economic Co-operation and Development. He was a Scot. We asked him if he felt that the work of the OECD had progressed in those years.

"Not at all," he answered.

"Why not?"

Without hesitation he replied, "Because it's impossible for the French and the British ever to agree on anything."

Splendid encouragement for the start of our life together! It is true that there is no lack of points of divergence. What my husband ecstatically calls good fresh air, to me is a nasty draught. We have fought the battle of tea and coffee, and ended in a compromise. The English instinctively mistrust theories and believe only in action. The French see no sense in action unless it is backed by a coherent theory. As Salvador de Madariaga so shrewdly observes in his book *Englishmen, Frenchmen, Spaniards*, "English thought is concrete and vague, and French thought is abstract and precise."[2] All this has taken us a bit of working out, but we have been amused to discover that, behind these appearances, our basic human nature is in fact the same. We now know that between a Frenchman — or in this case a Frenchwoman — who does not always have to be right and an Englishman who accepts that perhaps he needs other people's help, a co-operation can be established of the sort that the world badly needs.

Our differences and possibilities have been spotlighted for us by our own contacts with Africa. France and Britain started colonising from diametrically opposite points of view. The French considered that, from Tunis to Dakar to Libreville, the greatest gift they could offer an African was to transform him into a nice little Frenchman. It never occurred to the British that anyone else could possibly become British. But behind these two attitudes lies the same pride, whose bitter fruits we are reaping today. I am not forgetting those men and women who sacrificed the whole of their lives in the service of distant continents. They suffered loneliness, fever, hunger, persecution and privation to offer a little brotherhood, and their shining example lives in thousands of hearts. But the selfishness of the majority has done its best to obscure that light. Our greed for ivory, for gold, for an easy life where you could be "somebody" on the cheap, all this has nearly obliterated the heroic selflessness of the few. There, too, the golden threads and the blood-red threads have been inextricably intertwined.

What can we do?

First, we can remember that the real Europe is not cars, motorways, hospitals and schools, but values — brotherly compassion, integrity, a sense of justice, a love of freedom. In the midst of crisis, dogged by inflation or unemployment, we can still revive those values which are the treasure that the world wants of us. Then we must complete the process of reconciliation. We must sweep away the prejudices inherited from past centuries; we must learn to understand and, more than that, to love the ways of thought and the ways of life of those people who live on the other side of the mountains, the other side of the great river, the other side of the sea. And we must practise towards other continents the policy of the humble and open heart — nothing to do with subservience, everything to do with the equality we talk so much about.

It is a fact that women have a particular role to play in all these areas which go so far beyond the material side of life. It is an act of faith to believe that this role can be decisive. One woman who has made this act of faith is Saidie Patterson, President of "Women Together" in Ireland. She began life in a setting straight out of Dickens, one of a large family where work began at the age of five, the children threading needles, their mother hemming handkerchiefs and napkins. Out of these sordid houses came the finest damask tablecloths; their inhabitants ate off newspapers, and hardly ever ate their fill. Saidie was one of the first to organise the women textile workers in her country. She has all the fire of the Irish, but what shines from her is not hatred of a system, but love — a personal, practical love for each of the thousands of women she is responsible for. Now, in the present troubles, this love has spread even more widely. She writes:

" 'Women Together' was founded . . . after a cleaner in the Belfast Gas Works had a persistent dream that the women of Northern Ireland were uniting to tell the violent ones: 'Put away your guns and your bombs, give us back peace.'. . .

"We have a single message: If you face a wall of hate, climb it with help in your hands and hope in your heart. And this is what we have been doing these past four years. . ."

One story illustrates how they climb these walls:

"Our streets were in a mess. . . A Roman Catholic road sweeper would be afraid to go into a Protestant area or a Protestant into a Roman Catholic area. We felt a dirty street was a beaten street, so we persuaded our neighbours to sweep with us.

"Die-hards on both sides were suspicious. They asked, 'Who gave you permission to sweep?' We replied that those were our streets. We edged closer to the battle-field. . .

"As rioters traded bricks and petrol bombs with rubber bullets of the Army, we linked arms and spanned the streets holding our ground against missiles and jeers. Mothers advanced arm in arm scattering the youngsters home; soldiers watched in wonder at a weapon more powerful than any they carried."[3]

With that sort of courage there is nothing that the women of Europe could not undertake.

Notes
[1] Leif Hovelsen: *Out of the Evil Night*, Blandford, 1959.
[2] Salvador de Madariaga: *Englishmen, Frenchmen, Spaniards*, Pitman, 1969, p. 74.
[3] *New World News*, London, 19 July 1975.

14

Suffering

Life brings gifts of light and gifts of darkness. The gifts of light — good business, good health, good school reports — pose no problem. For most of us, happiness is normal and we rarely take time to stop and marvel at it.

When the gifts of darkness come, the picture changes completely. There are at once a thousand questions: "Why me? Why now? Why this? If there is a God, how can he allow this to happen to me? Why? Why?" Job, that legendary man of misfortune, speaks only in questions: "Why does God give sufferers light, and life to men in bitter despair, who long for death, and long in vain, who dig for it more than buried treasure?"[1] Many philosophers since the author of the Book of Job have applied themselves to the problem of suffering. But is there a universal solution?

In fact, suffering is always some person's suffering. It is the Smiths, who have lost their eldest daughter in a car accident. It is Joan, whose husband has left her for another woman. It is Ted, a conscientious and hardworking man, who has lost his job because of the economic situation. It is Mary, mother of a young family, who has just discovered that she has multiple sclerosis. It is each of these people, and nobody else, who has to find an answer that satisfies their inmost spirit. And the answer may be different for each person.

Suffering is indeed so subjective that it is impossible to judge anyone else's. A North American Indian proverb says: "Never judge a man until you have walked in his moccasins for a fortnight." Our shoulders are not equally strong for carrying burdens. A trifle for one person is a tragedy for another. And we all know people who suffer in a real way from completely imaginary illnesses. One witty woman, conscious of this failing, said to a friend at the end of her life, "Oh, my dear, I've had so many unhappinesses — and half of them never happened!"

All of us, some day or other, meet suffering on our way. And from the child who has had a bump to the adult in distress, those who need consolation turn to us. I am conscious of not knowing what to say about the "why" of suffering. But I do know that by reading, by watching other people facing their own trials, I have gradually been able to discover in mine a guiding thread, not a "why" but a "what for".

In certain cases, we have clearly brought misfortune on our own heads. In others, tragedy is the result of another person's cruelty. I know a remarkable Irish woman whose twenty-year-old son was killed in one of the shootings which are, sadly, commonplace in her country. In the midst of her sorrow, this woman was faced with the alternatives of forgiving or taking revenge. Revenge was tempting, but she knew that it would add another twist to the vicious circle of violence. She decided to forgive, and took time and trouble to meet the young extremists of the opposing party to try, using her acceptance of suffering and her love for Ireland, to offer them a more constructive revolution.

Hers keeps company with thousands of such bereavements all over the world. They are the same, whether the people doing the shooting belong to "regular" or "irregular" forces. The hole torn in the family is of the same size. One day, from the heart of all this suffering, perhaps women may bring to birth the will to solve problems by means other than violence. I use the word "will" deliberately. It is quite a different thing from lip service to a vague ideal. The uncountable capital of unjust suffering, which increases every day, could become the means to change the world.

Sometimes, when suffering comes, all these factors seem to be involved — our own weaknesses, the ill-will of others, fate. And sometimes, fate alone seems to be at work. I hope I may be forgiven for using myself as an example here. I think it is the most useful thing I can do.

I feel that I have been very lucky. Like everyone else, I have had my ups and downs, but none of those major disasters that blacken life. Besides, I am by nature an optimist. I have enjoyed what has fallen to my lot, and not wasted time in fruitless regrets about what might have been. And I am conscious of belonging, in many ways, to a privileged minority of mankind.

In the course of last year, I had certain digestive troubles which did not seem serious and which never stopped any of my activities. But just before the school holidays, as a safety measure I consulted a specialist. Within a week I was in hospital and under the care of a surgeon. I made his assistant promise to tell me the whole truth. The verdict fell like a guillotine: inoperable cancer.

To meet the initial shock, the human psyche has certain resources. It takes its own time to accept the inevitable, and begins by believing against all the evidence that it is possible to go back to "before". Then you can talk, you can weep if need be, you are sustained by the simple courage of other patients in the ward who have been through the same ordeal a few days earlier. You are surrounded by the first affectionate messages of your family.

But the moment comes when you must face reality. The flood of "whys" pours into your mind. All the possibilities whirl around: death, separation, physical suffering; fear of the unknown, hope of a cure. A few thoughts — if that is the right word: I can find no other — allowed me to keep my peace of mind or to find it again in the midst of this turmoil.

I did not try to resist fear. It is too inherent in human nature in a situation like that. It was better to let it break over me in waves without fighting back.

Self-pity was quite a different matter. I remembered a young woman of my acquaintance who, some fifteen years ago, had found herself in the same situation as mine. She was recently married, and had a little boy of two and a half. Despite all her efforts, she could not regain her peace of heart. And the weeks that went by, perhaps the last of her life, were poisoned by bitterness. One of her friends, an older woman, wise and compassionate, decided to tackle the problem head-on. It was so difficult that she stood for ten minutes outside the door before she dared to knock. Then she went in and asked, "When are you going to stop being sorry for yourself?" It was like a well-placed lancet at the heart of an abscess. There was a long silence. Then the young woman's face lit up in a smile and she replied, "Now." The respite in her illness that followed did not last, but her final months were illumined by a light that shone long after her death.

I realised that when I felt bitter and rebellious, it was not so much for objective reasons — though there was no lack of them — but because self-pity made them seem worse.

One certainty has accompanied me all through these days, and stays with me like a rock. I can only express it in the phrase: "God never makes a mistake." What happens to me is never the result of carelessness or misdirection on the part of Providence. I am not saying that God ever wants illness, suffering or death for anyone. Christ devoted too large a part of his time on earth to curing the sick and raising the dead for one to believe that. The author of Revelations in describing Paradise uses a very vivid expression: "And God shall wipe away all tears from their eyes."[2] But in the world as it is at present, in the midst of turbulence and evolution, God allows certain evils to touch us. Why? This remains incomprehensible to us. But he does have that extraordinary power which enables him to draw good out of evil. On that we can rely.

However, the human mind is so made that it needs, if not an explanation, at least a deep sense of meaning. That brought me to the heart of the question. Little by little, the conviction came to me that the purpose of suffering is inseparable from the purpose of life. If I know why I am alive, I will know why I suffer. I shall perhaps be incapable of putting it into words, but my whole being will be at peace.

The purpose of life has to be sufficiently vast and deep to include everything. An illustration comes to my mind which, if it makes me smile today, seemed to me rather bitter when I was first in hospital. A year ago for the first time in our lives, thanks to two legacies, we were able to buy our first home and, a fortnight before my operation, our first car. We had never lacked a roof nor transport when we needed them, but if you have waited until you are fifty to own your first house and your first car, it rather goes to your head. If the meaning of life lies in enjoying material things, then the situation was particularly distressing. That Mediterranean-blue Peugeot was really their symbol. My resentment, needless to say, did not last long and, besides the journeys between home and hospital, my husband and I have been able to enjoy two or three unforgettable drives in a particularly mild and luminous late autumn.

In the hurly-burly of daily existence you scarcely take time to stop and think about the purpose of life. You are too taken up with living. Now, in the sleepless hours of the night and the long hours of inactivity by day, I have more time to think than I have ever had. It seems to me that my life on earth has three aims: the fulfilment of certain tasks; allowing my character to become, some would say more human, others would say nearer to the divine; and the third, the one that is perhaps most on my heart, doing honour to my Creator.

As to the fulfilment of tasks, we ourselves are the worst judges of what they are. The world is teeming with people who think they are indispensable, while their colleagues, their families, their neighbours hold a rather different opinion. It is, in any case, usually only after the event that we realise that we have been of some use. And in the final analysis, it is not up to us to judge when our task is completed. I read somewhere: "As long as my task is unfinished, I am immortal." It is up to someone greater than ourselves to decide.

In the mysterious process of character building, it is certain that suffering plays a considerable part from the moment that it is accepted with good grace. Perhaps this is what François Mauriac meant when he said to his son: "I am uneasy about the limited part that you allow suffering to play in your life."[3] Excessive self-confidence, the feeling that you do not need others, pride, the inability to feel compassion, all these can be thoroughly ploughed up by suffering. So too can activism, indifference, superficiality.

St James says it better than anyone at the beginning of his Epistle: "When all kinds of trials and temptations crowd into your lives, my brothers, don't resent them as intruders, but welcome them as friends. Realise that they come to test your faith and to produce in you the quality of endurance. But let the process go on until that endurance is fully developed, and you will find you have become men of mature character with the right sort of independence." Knowing that he is suggesting something difficult, he adds: "And if, in the process, any of you does not know how to meet any particular problem, he has only to ask God — who gives generously to all men without making them feel foolish or guilty — and he may be quite sure that the necessary wisdom will be given him."[4]

"Let the process go on until the endurance is fully developed. . ." That is a truth I very much need, and that is what these tests bring, not in their initial shock but in their daily reality. I am one of those women who like to take hold of the future with well thought-out plans, and not knowing what lies ahead of me is teaching me an availability, reborn each day, which I believe I greatly needed to find.

Then there is the third aim: to do honour to my Creator by the way I live. That aim more than any other is altered not a jot by health or sickness, by success or failure, by prosperity or poverty, or by any outside circumstance. We ourselves decide our attitude in the face of trial. The popular expression "He must bear his cross", when it is applied to a misfortune that has not been chosen, has always seemed to me singularly inappropriate; to encounter unhappiness is only the simple proof that we are human. But if we decide, for the love of other people and for the love of God, to accept in the midst of our difficulties the gifts of joy, of peace, of patience, then indeed we can begin to speak of the cross. The Man who first carried it did so because of a costly decision, freely taken in obedience and love. It is only when we have done all we can to follow him that we can begin to use that word.

There is one thing more — our attitude to the suffering of others. Today we are made conscious of it with an intensity which no other age has known. No drought in Somalia, earthquake in Turkey, civil war in Angola, famine in Bangladesh can happen without its horror penetrating to our living-rooms. These intolerable sights produce a natural reflex of self-defence, which tempts us to harden into indifference. Besides, what can we do? We can't make rain over the Sahara, stop the earth quaking, reconcile peoples at the other end of the world who have decided to kill each other. And social injustice batters at our own doors. Slums do not exist only in Rio de Janeiro, Mexico, Calcutta — we have them in our own European cities.

Such suffering can be exploited for political ends. It can be used to prove that someone else's way of doing things is wrong and ours is right. It can only be cured by people who have nothing to prove, nothing to gain and no one to hate — people whose only enemies are injustice and misery.

Mother Teresa of Calcutta, whose Sisters of Charity care for the outcast and dying, approaches suffering with the attitude of the saints. Malcolm Muggeridge's book about her, *Something Beautiful for God*, has in it a passage which draws together our own suffering and that of others — which in the end are one:

"Accompanying Mother Teresa to these different activities for the purpose of filming them — to the Home for the Dying, to the lepers and unwanted children, I found I went through three phases. The first was horror mixed with pity, the second compassion pure and simple, and the third, reaching far beyond compassion, something I had never experienced before — an awareness that these dying and derelict men and women, these lepers with stumps instead of hands, these unwanted children, were not pitiable, repulsive or forlorn, but rather dear and delightful; as it might be, friends of long standing, brothers and sisters."[5]

"Dear and delightful. . ." These words have remained in my mind like a triumphant echo to our poor "whys". No, suffering is not absurd.

Notes
[1] Job 3, 20-21 (Moffatt's translation).
[2] Revelations 21, 4 (Authorised Version).
[3] Claude Mauriac: *Les Espaces imaginaires*, Grasset, 1975, p. 62.
[4] James 1, 2-5 (J.B. Phillips' translation).
[5] Malcolm Muggeridge: *Something Beautiful for God*, Collins/Fontana, 1972, p. 52.

15

Tomorrow

A doctor recently addressed the Parents' Association of my son's school. He said, "In the last analysis, men usually realise the secret dreams of their mothers." And he supported this assertion with examples from history and from his personal experience.

The remark seemed to me too true to be comfortable. What then were my secret dreams for my son? To be a success in life, to have a good standard of living, to be happy, to have a stable character, to serve others, to contribute towards rebuilding the world? Did my dreams need to be brought into the daylight, shaken out and entirely reshaped?

Later I understood that beneath that remark lay an even deeper meaning. We are the mothers of the world of tomorrow, and the reality of tomorrow's world will be what we have secretly dreamed today. "Secret dreams" is another way of saying "what we really want", "what we are really committed to".

I see three possible alternatives. We can dream of ease and success for ourselves — easier work, easier husband, easier material life. I believe that in this case the result is inevitable: the world of tomorrow will be drowned in a tide of materialism more devastating still than the pollution that threatens our planet.

Or we can dream of a world of more justice and more brotherhood, but one that conforms to our own ideas and to the ideas of those who think as we do; and we condemn the world to become a battle-field of opposing factions that will in the end destroy it.

Or else we can dream of a world free of hate, fear and greed; where no one exploits or dominates anyone else; where each person is guided by his own deepest inner conviction and so finds liberty and discipline; a world where Christians, who have so often prayed "Thy will be done on earth as it is in heaven", make of this prayer the shining reality of their lives.

You may say that all this applies to men as much as to women. That is not entirely true. To a certain extent it is for men to do, for women to be. If we compete to the bitter end with men on the field of action, there will be no one left to have vision and to nourish it in the heart of mankind. Action will no longer have roots and will become confusion. Ruskin wrote: "There is not a war in the world, no, nor an injustice, but you women are answerable for it; not in that you have provoked, but in that you have not hindered. . . There is no suffering, no injustice, no misery in the earth, but the guilt of it lies with you."[1]

If women clean the house, says the proverb, men will wipe their feet on the door-mat. This is expressed in another way in a book aptly entitled *Being and Doing*: "As long as the women of England refuse to guide and inspire, as long as they forget their nature, and think of pleasure instead of blessing, as long as they shut their ears to the agony of the cities of this land, that they may not be disturbed in their luxury, and literature, and art, so long will men, as they have ever done, take the impulse of their lives from them, and do nothing chivalrous, nothing really self-sacrificing, nothing very noble and persistent, for the blessing of the world.

"The regeneration of society is in the power of the woman, and she turns away from it.

"All future English generations might call her blessed, and she prefers to be called fashionable."[2]

This text was published in Liverpool in 1912. It still moves me by its relevance. Replace our great-grandmothers' desire to be fashionable by our modern passion to be "with it", replace the poverty of the English towns at the beginning of the century by the needs of the Third World in the last quarter of the century, and there is not another word that needs changing.

We have explored a lot of ground together, and the moment is coming for each to continue the adventure for herself. I like to think that we have before us a landscape with a wide horizon. There may be mountains to climb, cliffs to scale. There are also flowers beside the stream and, for each, a path to follow which is her own.

We are not isolated individuals, lost in the mass, powerless. We are the possessors, on the contrary, of immense power, which we choose to use day after day for good or for evil.

There lies our freedom.

Notes
[1] John Ruskin: *Sesame and Lilies*, para 91, George Allen, 1905, p. 140.
[2] Constance M. Whishaw: *Being and Doing*, Edward Howell, Liverpool, 1912, pp. 168-9.